DAY HIKES AROUND
MISSOULA
MONTANA

by Robert Stone

Day Hike Books, Inc.
RED LODGE, MONTANA

Published by Day Hike Books, Inc.
P.O. Box 865
Red Lodge, Montana 59068

Distributed by The Globe Pequot Press
246 Goose Lane
P.O. Box 480
Guilford, CT 06437-0480
800-243-0495 (direct order) · 800-820-2329 (fax order)
www.globe-pequot.com

Photographs by Robert Stone
Design by Paula Doherty

The author has made every attempt to provide accurate
information in this book. However, trail routes and features may
change—please use common sense and forethought, and be mindful
of your own capabilities. Let this book guide you, but be aware
that each hiker assumes responsibility for their own safety.
The author and publisher do not assume any responsibility for loss,
damage or injury caused through the use of this book.

Cover photo: Waterfall in Blodgett Canyon, Hike 46
Back cover photo: Looking across Holland Lake
to the Mission Mountains, Hike 49

Table of Contents

THE HIKES

Rattlesnake National Recreation Area and Sawmill — Curry Trail System

Mount Jumbo Recreation Area

In the town of Missoula

Mount Sentinel and Pattee Canyon Recreation Area

Blue Mountain Recreation Area

Ninemile Ranger Station
and Fish Creek Road

Highway 12: Lolo over Lolo Pass into Idaho

Bitterroot Mountains and Valley

Seeley — Swan Valley

Rock Creek Drainage and Welcome Creek

About Missoula and the Hikes

Missoula is rich in character and diversity with a wide variety of museums, art galleries, boutiques, restaurants, a university, musical and cultural events, as well as being encircled by picturesque scenery and many hiking trails. The town was first settled in the 1860s. It grew rapidly as a mining and logging center with the arrival of the railroad. It is now the third largest city in Montana and an active university town. Missoula has a beautiful historic commercial district with turn-of-the-century architecture. The historic residential district is near the university. The University of Montana, on the banks of the Clark Fork River, is located near the base of Mount Sentinel by the mouth of Hellgate Canyon.

At an elevation of 3,205 feet and surrounded by mountains, Missoula sits at the hub of five merging valleys—the Bitterroot from the south, the Mission from the north, the Blackfoot and Hellgate from the east and the Missoula from the west. Three rivers—the Bitterroot, the Blackfoot and the Clark Fork—are in or within a few miles of the city. A short distance in any direction leads to national forests and wilderness areas.

Missoula is surrounded by the two-million-acre Lolo National Forest. The Lolo National Forest has an abundance of wildlife, including black bear, grizzly, moose, deer, big horn sheep, mountain goats, wolves and elk. The forest also has 350,000 acres of winter elk range. The land is rich with ponderosa pine, lodgepole pine, Douglas fir, subalpine fir and western larch. The Lolo National Forest provides access into four wilderness areas and a variety of recreational areas. Four miles southeast of Missoula is the Pattee Canyon Recreation Area. Two miles southwest is the Blue Mountain Recreation Area. Less than four miles north is the Rattlesnake National Recreation Area. Much of the area is set aside for preservation as wilderness.

Rattlesnake Creek, Missoula's watershed, flows through the canyon's narrow valley floor. The drainage is fed by more than fifty smaller creeks. Within this area are eight different trailheads with a network of interconnecting trails. The trails follow a several creeks and gulches through alpine and subalpine landscape. The glacially carved topography is home to 7,000-foot summits, hanging valleys, cirques and more than thirty lakes.

To the south of Missoula, along Highway 93, is the Bitterroot Valley. The Bitterroot River carved this twenty-mile wide valley that sits at an elevation of 3,000 feet. This fertile valley is nestled between two mountain ranges—the Bitterroot Mountains and the Sapphire Mountains.

To the west of the valley are the dramatic Bitterroot Mountains. The Bitterroots straddle the Continental Divide and form the Montana/Idaho border. The northern portion of the range is among Montana's wettest areas, receiving more than 100 inches of moisture annually. The Bitterroot Range is known for its jagged 9,000-foot granite peaks and deep canyons. The fourteen canyons are also creek drainages with headwaters from alpine lakes. These precipitous canyon walls rise 5,000 feet from the valley floor in only three miles. The Bitterroot National Forest encompasses 1.6 million acres, with about half the forest as protected wilderness area. The Bitterroot Mountains have an extensive 1,600-mile trail system, including the Nez Perce Trail, route of the tragic flight in 1877, and the historic Lewis and Clark Trail. Hikes 37—48 are found within the Bitterroot Valley. (The fires of 2000 were centered in Blodgett Canyon in the Bitterroot Valley west of Hamilton.)

To the east of the Bitterroot Valley are the molten slopes of the Sapphire Mountains. The wild Sapphire Range has 98,000 acres of designated wilderness, including the Welcome Creek Wilderness. With narrow canyons and steep ridges, the main artery of the Welcome Creek Wilderness is Rock Creek, a "blue ribbon" rated trout fishing creek.

To the northeast of Missoula, along Highway 83, is the glacially carved Seeley-Swan Valley. This ten-mile wide corridor extends for eighty miles with two beautiful rivers—the

Clearwater River flowing into the Blackfoot River and the Swan River flowing into Flathead Lake. The valley is bordered to the west for thirty miles by the majestic snow-capped Mission Mountains. To the valley's east is the Swan Mountain Range, offering access into the Bob Marshall Wilderness, the Scapegoat Wilderness and the Great Bear Wilderness. Along the valley and its bordering mountain ranges are hundreds of pristine lakes. With over 400 miles of hiking trails, dozens of campgrounds, resorts, guest ranches and easy access to the back country, the Seeley-Swan Valley is a recreational haven.

This guide focuses on 55 hikes of various lengths in and around Missoula. They range from easy to moderately strenuous and have been chosen for their scenery, variety and ability to be hiked within the day. To help you decide which hikes are most appealing to you, a brief summary of the highlights is included with each hike. The hikes are also accompanied with their own maps and detailed driving and hiking directions. You may enjoy these areas for a short time or the whole day.

If you wish to extend your hike into the backcountry, the trails are also detailed on an assortment of commercial maps. These include the U.S. Geological Survey topographical maps, the U.S. Forest Service Selway-Bitterroot National Forest map and the U.S. Forest Service Lolo National Forest map. The relevant maps are listed with each hike and can be purchased at most area sporting goods stores.

Be sure to wear supportive, comfortable hiking shoes and be prepared for inclement weather. The elevation for these hikes can be as high as 8,000 feet. At this altitude the air can be cool. Afternoon thundershowers are common throughout the summer. Be prepared for unpredictable weather by wearing layered clothing and packing a warm hat. A rain poncho, sunscreen, mosquito repellent, a snack and drinking water are highly recommended.

Enjoy your hikes as you discover the beautiful valleys and forests that surround Missoula.

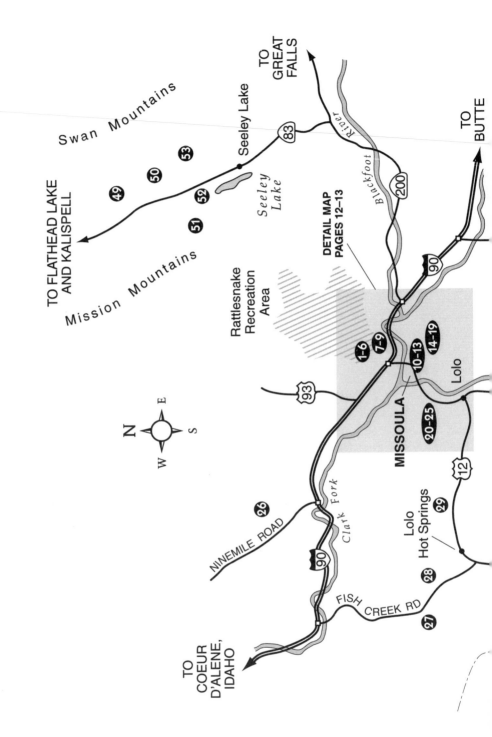

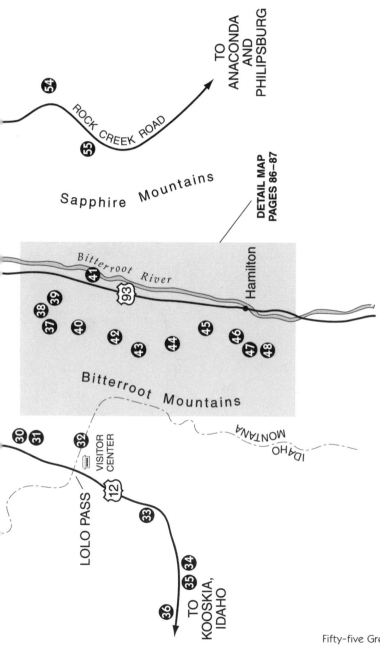

MAP OF THE HIKES

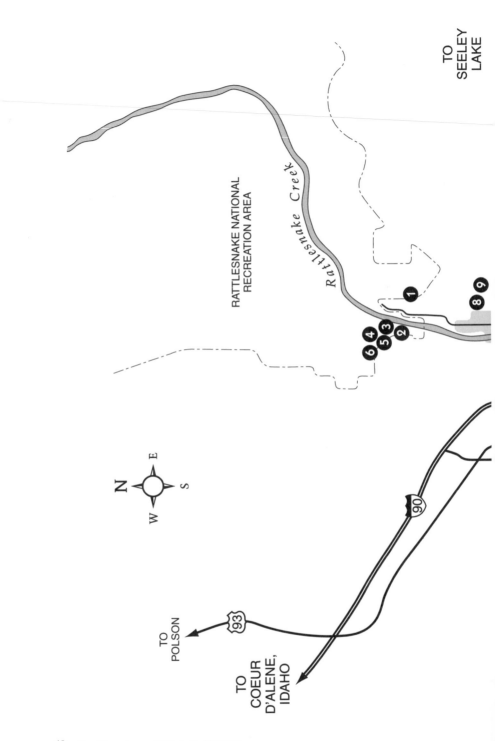

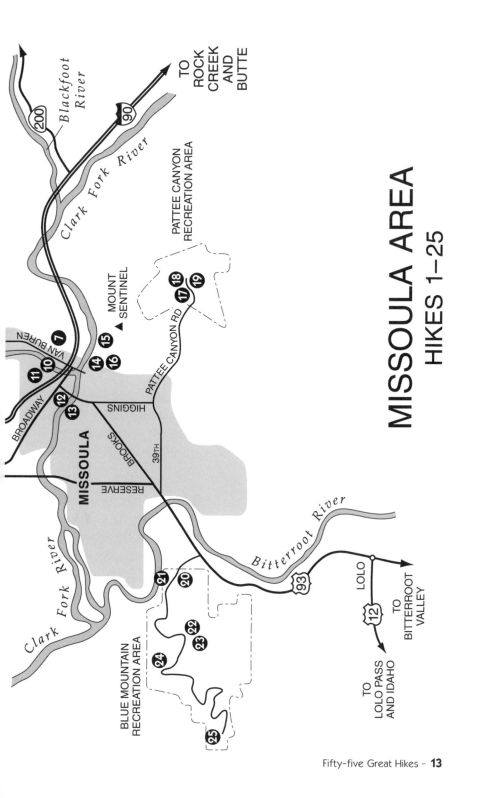

MISSOULA AREA
HIKES 1–25

Hike 1
Woods Gulch
Rattlesnake National Recreation Area

Hiking distance: 3 miles round trip
Hiking time: 1.5 hours
Elevation gain: 800 feet
Maps: U.S.G.S. Northeast Missoula
Rattlesnake Nat'l. Recreation Area and Wilderness map
Mount Jumbo Area Recreation Plan map

Summary of hike: Woods Gulch is a lush, streamside canyon near the southern boundary of the Rattlesnake National Recreation Area. The 11-mile Sheep Mountain Trail ascends through Woods Gulch, following the stream drainage in a ponderosa and lodgepole pine forest. This hike takes the first 1.5 miles to a ridge. From the ridge are great views of Marshall Canyon and the Marshall Ski Area.

Driving directions: From I-90 in Missoula, take the Van Buren Street exit and head 4.1 miles north to Woods Gulch Road and turn right. (Van Buren Street turns into Rattlesnake Drive.) Continue 0.5 miles to the signed trailhead on the left. Park in the pullouts on the left.

Hiking directions: Head east past the trail sign and up the forested gulch along the south side of the creek. At a quarter mile is the first of two consecutive creek crossings. Continue steadily uphill 1.5 miles to the top of Woods Gulch. At the ridge is a trail junction. The Sheep Mountain Trail follows the ridge to the left, reaching Blue Point at 5 miles and Sheep Mountain at 10 miles. The right fork connects with the Ridge Trail into the Mount Jumbo Recreation Area. Both directions have a gentle grade, are well-defined, and worth exploring. Return back down Woods Gulch.

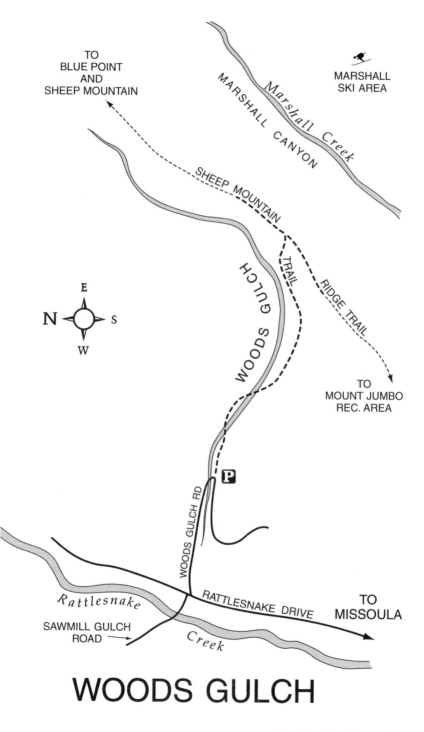

TO
BLUE POINT
AND
SHEEP MOUNTAIN

MARSHALL
SKI AREA

MARSHALL CANYON

Marshall Creek

SHEEP MOUNTAIN

TRAIL

RIDGE TRAIL

WOODS GULCH

E
N — S
W

TO
MOUNT JUMBO
REC. AREA

P

WOODS GULCH RD

Rattlesnake

RATTLESNAKE DRIVE

TO
MISSOULA

SAWMILL GULCH
ROAD →

Creek

WOODS GULCH

Hike 2
Main Rattlesnake Trail
Rattlesnake National Recreation Area

Hiking distance: 6 miles round trip
Hiking time: 3 hours
Elevation gain: 400 feet
Maps: U.S.G.S. Northeast Missoula
   Rattlesnake Nat'l. Recreation Area and Wilderness map

Summary of hike: The 61,000-acre Rattlesnake National Recreation Area, part of the Lolo National Forest, is located at the northern city limits of Missoula. This spectacular area has sweeping mountains, hanging valleys, lake-filled basins and a large variety of orchids. There are eight separate trailheads, providing access to a web of interconnecting trails. The Main Rattlesnake Trail parallels Rattlesnake Creek up the main corridor of the glacially carved drainage basin.

Driving directions: From I-90 in Missoula, take the Van Buren Street exit and head 4.1 miles north to Sawmill Gulch Road on the left. (Van Buren Street turns into Rattlesnake Drive.) Turn left, crossing over Rattlesnake Creek, and continue 0.2 miles to the main trail parking lot on the right.

Hiking directions: Follow the main trail north past the trailhead sign. At a half mile is a junction with the Stuart Peak Trail on the left (Hikes 3 and 4) and a bridge over Rattlesnake Creek on the right. Continue straight ahead on the main trail another quarter mile, and take the smaller path to the right. This path stays close to the creek and reconnects with the main trail 1.7 miles from the trailhead. Continue following the main trail up canyon. At 2 miles, take the posted Wallman Trail to the left. Along the way are three trail forks. Take the right forks, rejoining the main trail. Return along the main trail, completing a double loop.

   To hike further, you may continue up canyon another half mile, descending into Poe Meadow.

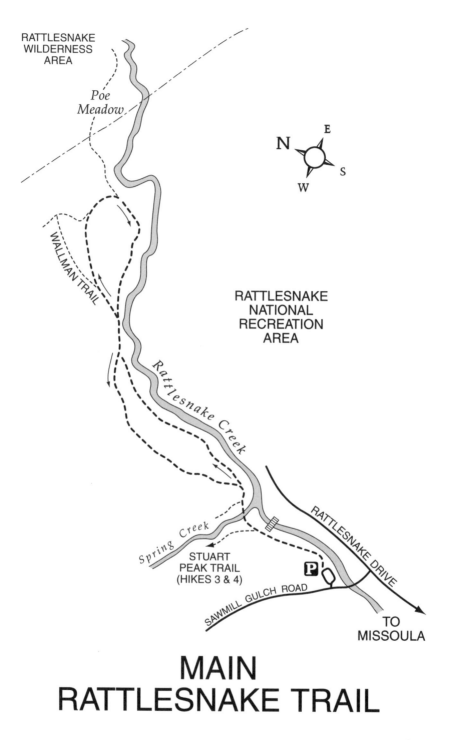

RATTLESNAKE
WILDERNESS
AREA

*Poe
Meadow*

WALLMAN TRAIL

Rattlesnake Creek

RATTLESNAKE
NATIONAL
RECREATION
AREA

N
E
W
S

Spring Creek

STUART
PEAK TRAIL
(HIKES 3 & 4)

RATTLESNAKE DRIVE

SAWMILL GULCH ROAD

TO
MISSOULA

MAIN
RATTLESNAKE TRAIL

Hike 3
Spring Creek Loop
Rattlesnake National Recreation Area

Hiking distance: 5.5 mile loop
Hiking time: 3 hours
Elevation gain: 450 feet
Maps: U.S.G.S. Northeast Missoula
Sawmill - Curry Trail System map
Rattlesnake Nat'l. Recreation Area and Wilderness map

Summary of hike: The Stuart Peak Trail heads up Spring Gulch parallel to Spring Creek. The Spring Creek Loop follows old cow paths and a farm lane, looping around both sides of the creek. Spring Creek empties into Rattlesnake Creek, a municipal watershed for Missoula.

Driving directions: From I-90 in Missoula, take the Van Buren Street exit and head 4.1 miles north to Sawmill Gulch Road on the left. (Van Buren Street turns into Rattlesnake Drive.) Turn left, crossing over Rattlesnake Creek, and continue 0.2 miles to the main trail parking lot on the right.

Hiking directions: From the parking lot, hike north past the trailhead signs. Take the Main Rattlesnake Trail (Hike 2) up the valley a half mile to the Stuart Peak Trail junction on the left. To the right is a bridge crossing over Rattlesnake Creek. Take the narrower Stuart Peak Trail heading upstream alongside Spring Creek. At the 1.3-mile marker is a log crossing over Spring Creek to the right for a shorter 2.6-mile loop. Continue north up Spring Gulch, passing the Curry Gulch Trail on the left (Hike 4). At 2.7 miles, as Spring Gulch narrows, is another trail junction. The left fork continues up the canyon to Stuart Peak, four miles further. Take the right fork, and cross a small wooden bridge over Spring Creek. Head downstream back to the Rattlesnake's main corridor, completing the loop. Take the trail to the right back to the trailhead.

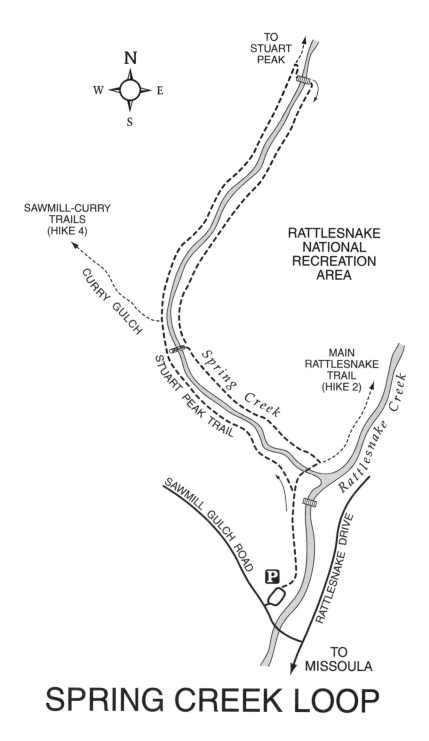

SPRING CREEK LOOP

Hike 4
Curry Gulch Trail to Curry Cabin
Rattlesnake National Recreation Area

Hiking distance: 4.8 miles round trip
Hiking time: 2.5 hours
Elevation gain: 400 feet
Maps: U.S.G.S. Northeast Missoula
Sawmill-Curry Trail System map
Rattlesnake Nat'l. Recreation Area and Wilderness map

Summary of hike: The Curry Cabin is a multi-room log cabin built in the late 1800s by Jacob Curry. At the cabin site are two additional log structures—an earth-covered root cellar and an old shed. The trail to the cabin follows the Main Rattlesnake corridor, then heads up through Spring Gulch and Curry Gulch.

Driving directions: From I-90 in Missoula, take the Van Buren Street exit and head 4.1 miles north to Sawmill Gulch Road and turn left. (Van Buren Street turns into Rattlesnake Drive.) Continue 0.2 miles, crossing over Rattlesnake Creek, to the main trail parking lot on the right.

Hiking directions: Head north a half mile up the Main Rattlesnake Trail, parallel to Rattlesnake Creek, to the signed Stuart Peak Trail on the left. To the right is a bridge crossing Rattlesnake Creek. Bear left up the forested draw along the left bank of Spring Creek. At the 1.3-mile marker is a log crossing over Spring Creek. Continue straight ahead 100 yards north to the signed Curry Gulch Trail. Go to the left, winding through the dense forest while steadily climbing up the drainage. One mile up Curry Gulch is a signed junction. The left fork leads to Sawmill Gulch (Hike 5). Take the right fork 200 yards to the Curry Cabin. After exploring the structures, return along the same trail to the cut-across trail at the 1.3-mile marker. Cross the logs over Spring Creek and return to the right along the east side of the creek, heading downstream to the Rattlesnake corridor. Go to the right, back to the trailhead.

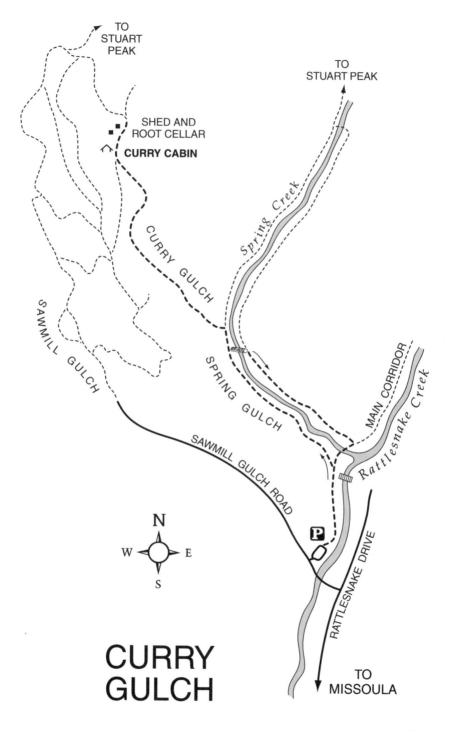

TO
STUART
PEAK

TO
STUART PEAK

SHED AND
ROOT CELLAR

CURRY CABIN

Spring Creek

CURRY GULCH

SAWMILL GULCH

SPRING GULCH

MAIN CORRIDOR

Rattlesnake Creek

SAWMILL GULCH ROAD

P

RATTLESNAKE DRIVE

N
W E
S

CURRY GULCH

TO
MISSOULA

Hike 5
Sawmill Gulch Loop
Rattlesnake National Recreation Area

Hiking distance: 2.6 mile loop
Hiking time: 1.5 hours
Elevation gain: 500 feet
Maps: U.S.G.S. Northeast Missoula
       Sawmill-Curry Trail System map
       Rattlesnake Nat'l. Recreation Area and Wilderness map

Summary of hike: Sawmill Gulch, part of the Curry Trail System, is a more recent addition (acquired in 1986) to the Rattlesnake National Recreation Area. The trails are quieter and less frequented than the Main Rattlesnake corridor. Many of these trails were originally made in the 1800s by prospectors, settlers and livestock. This trail follows a large meadow, passing remnants of some original ranch buildings. The Curry Trail System connects with Curry Gulch and the Spring Creek Trail (Hike 4).

Driving directions: From I-90 in Missoula, take the Van Buren Street exit and head 4.1 miles north to Sawmill Gulch Road and turn left. (Van Buren Street turns into Rattlesnake Drive.) Continue 1.4 miles, crossing over Rattlesnake Creek to the road's end. (At 1.2 miles is a road fork—stay to the right.)

Hiking directions: From the parking area, pass the gate and hike north towards the meadow. The trail follows the eastern edge of the meadow up the draw. Near the top, the remnants of the old ranch buildings are on the right. Just past the ranch site is a junction. Take the right fork up a narrow draw to a second junction. The left fork continues deeper into the Curry Trail System (see map for Hike 4). Take the right fork uphill along the eastern cliff edge, overlooking the meadow below. The trail winds through the forest to another junction. Again, take the right fork. The trail curves right and descends back to the meadow, completing the loop. Head left, back to the trailhead.

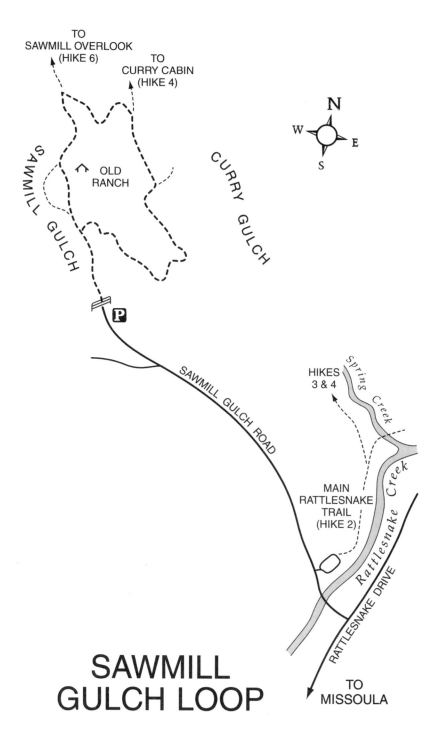

TO
SAWMILL OVERLOOK
(HIKE 6)

TO
CURRY CABIN
(HIKE 4)

N
W   E
S

SAWMILL GULCH

OLD
RANCH

CURRY GULCH

P

HIKES
3 & 4

Spring Creek

SAWMILL GULCH ROAD

MAIN
RATTLESNAKE
TRAIL
(HIKE 2)

Rattlesnake Creek

RATTLESNAKE DRIVE

SAWMILL
GULCH LOOP

TO
MISSOULA

Hike 6
Sawmill Gulch to Overlook
Rattlesnake National Recreation Area

Hiking distance: 3.8 mile loop
Hiking time: 2 hours
Elevation gain: 1,100 feet
Maps: U.S.G.S. Northeast Missoula
       Sawmill–Curry Trail System map
       Rattlesnake Nat'l. Recreation Area and Wilderness map

Summary of hike: This loop hike follows Sawmill Gulch and Curry Gulch through the winding forest terrain. The trail heads up a ridge to a 4,915-foot overlook. From the ridge are views north into the Rattlesnake Wilderness.

Driving directions: From I-90 in Missoula, take the Van Buren Street exit and head 4.1 miles north to Sawmill Gulch Road and turn left. (Van Buren Street turns into Rattlesnake Drive.) Continue 1.4 miles, crossing over Rattlesnake Creek to the road's end. (At 1.2 miles, stay to the right at the road fork.)

Hiking directions: Hike north past the gate on the old ranch road. Head up the draw across the east edge of the meadow. Pass the remnants of an old ranch to a junction and go to the right. Head up the narrow draw to a second junction. Bear left on the faint footpath, continuing uphill to another junction. Again, stay to the left, gaining more elevation until the trail connects with a wide, distinct path at the ridge. Bear right to a signed junction. Straight ahead, the Curry Trail heads northeast to the Stuart Peak Trail. Take the right fork on the narrow footpath, skirting the 4,915-foot overlook at the summit. Descend through the forest past various overlooks of Sawmill Gulch. Continue downhill, heading south past an intersecting trail from the left and another on the right. At the third junction bear right, following the contours of the mountain back to Sawmill Gulch. Complete the loop at the next junction. Take the left fork, returning through the meadow and past the old ranch.

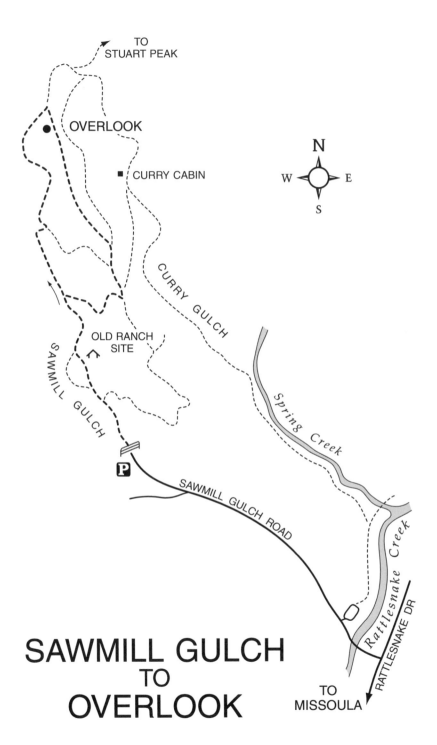

TO
STUART PEAK

OVERLOOK

CURRY CABIN

CURRY GULCH

OLD RANCH
SITE

SAWMILL GULCH

N
W   E
S

Spring Creek

Rattlesnake Creek

P

SAWMILL GULCH ROAD

RATTLESNAKE DR

TO
MISSOULA

SAWMILL GULCH
TO
OVERLOOK

Hike 7
L Trail
Mount Jumbo Recreation Area

Hiking distance: 1.5 miles round trip
Hiking time: 1 hour
Elevation gain: 500 feet
Maps: U.S.G.S. Southeast Missoula
      Mount Jumbo Area Recreation Plan map

Summary of hike: Mount Jumbo sits to the north of Mount Sentinel across from Hellgate Canyon and the Clark Fork River. The northern portion of Mount Jumbo Recreation Area is a winter range for elk and mule deer. It is closed to hikers through the beginning of May. The hike to the Loyola "L" in the southern portion of Mount Jumbo is open year around (weather permitting). The trail is less crowded than the University of Montana "M" Trail (Hike 16) with equally rewarding views of Missoula, the Rattlesnake Valley and the surrounding mountains.

Driving directions: From I-90 in Missoula, take the Van Buren Street exit and head one block north to Poplar Street—turn right. Continue three blocks to the trailhead on the left at the intersection of Poplar Street and Polk Street. Parking is available on both sides of the road.

Hiking directions: Head east up the hillside to an unpaved U.S. West access road. The left fork leads to another trailhead access at Cherry Street. Cross the road, picking up the footpath towards the "L," which can be seen up ahead. Continue to the ridge. Follow the edge of the hillside and cross the grassy flat. Begin the final steep ascent to the painted white rocks forming the "L." At the time of this writing, the formation was creatively enlarged to read "Lips." This is our turnaround spot.

To hike further, go left to the right angle of the "L" at a trail split. The right fork follows the vertical portion of the "L" and continues up to the 4,768-foot summit of Mount Jumbo. From here the Backbone Trail heads north to the Saddle Trail (Hike 8).

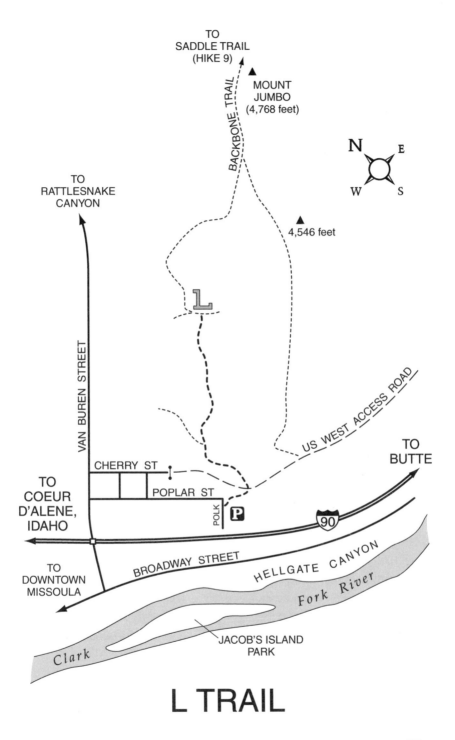

TO
SADDLE TRAIL
(HIKE 9)

MOUNT
JUMBO
(4,768 feet)

BACKBONE TRAIL

TO
RATTLESNAKE
CANYON

4,546 feet

N
E
W
S

L

US WEST ACCESS ROAD

VAN BUREN STREET

TO
BUTTE

CHERRY ST

TO
COEUR
D'ALENE,
IDAHO

POPLAR ST

POLK

P

I-90

TO
DOWNTOWN
MISSOULA

BROADWAY STREET

HELLGATE CANYON

Fork River

Clark

JACOB'S ISLAND
PARK

L TRAIL

Hike 8
North Loop Trail
Mount Jumbo Recreation Area

Hiking distance: 5 mile loop
Hiking time: 2.5 hours
Elevation gain: 800 feet
Maps: U.S.G.S. Northeast Missoula
         Mount Jumbo Area Recreation Plan map

Summary of hike: The North Loop Trail winds through the north region of Mount Jumbo Recreation Area, then makes connections with the Rattlesnake Recreation Area. This region is a winter range for mule deer and elk. It is closed to hikers throughout the winter until May 1. The trail, an old road, has a gentle grade and offers great views of Rattlesnake Canyon, Marshall Canyon and across the Missoula Valley.

Driving directions: From I-90 in Missoula, take the Van Buren Street exit, and head 2.1 miles north to Lincoln Hills Drive — turn right. (Van Buren Street turns into Rattlesnake Drive.) Continue 1.5 miles to the signed trailhead. Parking is available on both sides of the road.

Hiking directions: Head north past the trailhead map and up the grassy slope to a trail split. To the right is the Saddle Trail (Hike 9). Bear left, cross under the utility lines, and continue gradually uphill into a pine forest. At one mile the path leaves the forest and crosses the hillside. At the northwest point, loop back to the right and head southeast. Traverse the edge of the mountain up to the ridge and a junction. The left fork follows the Ridge Trail, connecting with the Sheep Mountain Trail and Woods Gulch (Hike 1). Bear to the right, heading south on the North Loop Trail. Descend through the forest above Marshall Canyon for a mile to a junction with the Saddle Trail. Bear right on the Saddle Trail, and cross the rolling slopes between the two peaks of Mount Jumbo. Continue past the Backbone Trail on the left. Complete the loop and return to the trailhead.

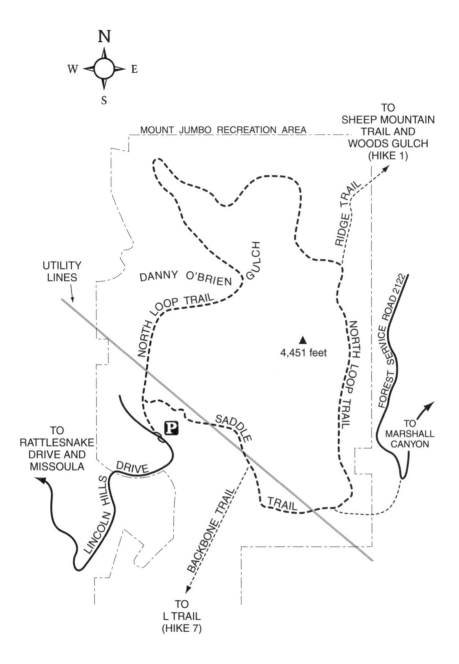

NORTH LOOP TRAIL

Hike 9
Saddle Trail
Mount Jumbo Recreation Area

Hiking distance: 3 miles round trip
Hiking time: 1.5 hours
Elevation gain: 300 feet
Maps: U.S.G.S. Northeast Missoula
　　　　Mount Jumbo Area Recreation Plan map

Summary of hike: The Saddle Trail crosses the saddle between the northern and southern peaks of Mount Jumbo. The trail connects Rattlesnake Canyon with Marshall Canyon, from Lincoln Hills Drive to Marshall Road. The Saddle Trail also connects with the North Loop Trail (Hike 8) and the Backbone Trail to the "L" (Hike 7).

Driving directions: From I-90 in Missoula, take the Van Buren Street exit, and head 2.1 miles north to Lincoln Hills Drive —turn right. (Van Buren Street turns into Rattlesnake Drive.) Continue 1.5 miles to the signed trailhead. Parking is available on both sides of the road.

Hiking directions: Pass the trailhead map and head north across the grassy hillside. At 0.1 mile is a junction just before reaching the utility lines. The left fork is the North Loop Trail (Hike 8). Take the right fork on the Saddle Trail. Head gently uphill, crossing the rolling hills and meadows. At the second pass under the utility poles is the Backbone Trail, bearing to the right and leading to the "L." Continue on the Saddle Trail, curving left and heading east. Cross the rolling slopes through the tree-dotted meadow by a vernal pool. At 1.1 mile is a junction. To the left is the North Loop Trail leading up to the Ridge Trail and Woods Gulch (Hike 1). Go right, traversing the hillside above the Clark Fork River and Hellgate Canyon to the gated Mount Jumbo boundary and gate. The trail descends 0.2 miles to Forest Service Road 2122, a connector road to Marshall Canyon. Return by retracing your steps.

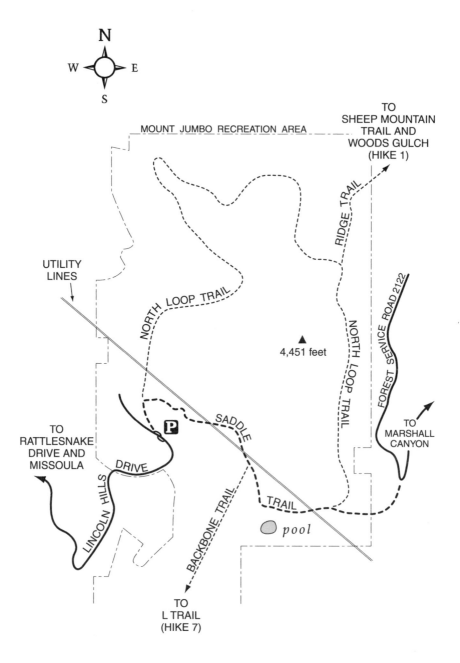

W
N
E
S

MOUNT JUMBO RECREATION AREA

TO
SHEEP MOUNTAIN
TRAIL AND
WOODS GULCH
(HIKE 1)

RIDGE TRAIL

UTILITY
LINES

NORTH LOOP TRAIL

NORTH LOOP TRAIL

FOREST SERVICE ROAD 2122

▲
4,451 feet

P

SADDLE

TO
MARSHALL
CANYON

TO
RATTLESNAKE
DRIVE AND
MISSOULA

LINCOLN HILLS

DRIVE

BACKBONE TRAIL

TRAIL

pool

TO
L TRAIL
(HIKE 7)

SADDLE TRAIL

Hike 10
Bolle Birdwatching Trail
Greenough Park

Hiking distance: 1 mile loop
Hiking time: 30 minutes
Elevation gain: Level
Maps: U.S.G.S. Northeast Missoula
Trails Missoula booklet

Summary of hike: Greenough Park has hiking paths that wind along Rattlesnake Creek as it flows through this 42-acre park at the mouth of the Rattlesnake Valley. The park is a bird habitat donated to the City of Missoula in 1902 by the Greenough Family. The gift included a provision that the land would be "forever maintained in its natural state." Several information stations about birds are located along the path. As many as 120 varieties of birds have been known to inhabit the area. Greenough Park has mature ponderosa pine trees, cotton-woods and lush riparian vegetation along Rattlesnake Creek. Benches and picnic tables are available.

Driving directions: From I-90 in Missoula, take the Van Buren Street exit, and drive 0.3 miles north to Locust Street on the left. Turn left, and continue 2 blocks to Monroe Street. The parking lot is on the west side of Monroe Street.

Hiking directions: From the parking lot, head to the bridge over Rattlesnake Creek. Once over the bridge, take the path to the right, hiking clockwise around the loop. (To the left is a short loop around a grassy picnic area by the creek.) The trail along the west side of Rattlesnake Creek is paved. At 0.4 miles, the trail crosses over the creek via a bridge to a foot trail on the right. The return trail is a natural path through a shady forest on the east bank of the creek. The trail follows Rattlesnake Creek back to the parking lot.

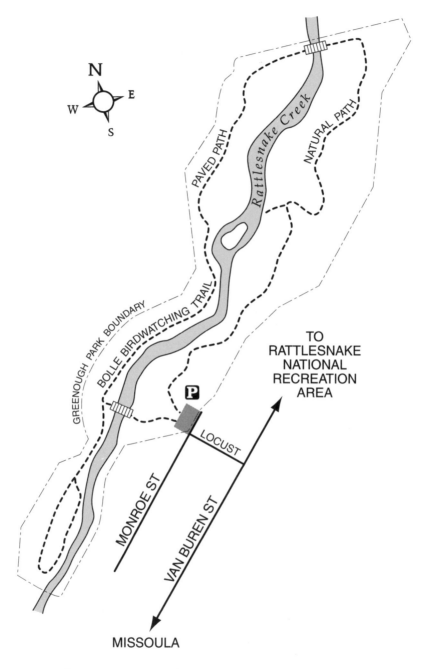

N
E
W
S

Rattlesnake Creek

PAVED PATH

NATURAL PATH

GREENOUGH PARK BOUNDARY

BOLLE BIRDWATCHING TRAIL

P

TO
RATTLESNAKE
NATIONAL
RECREATION
AREA

LOCUST

MONROE ST

VAN BUREN ST

MISSOULA

GREENOUGH PARK

Hike 11
Waterworks Hill to Peace Sign

Hiking distance: 2.2 miles round trip
Hiking time: 1 hour
Elevation gain: 450 feet
Maps: U.S.G.S. Northeast Missoula

Summary of hike: Waterworks Hill is a forgotten gem in the city of Missoula. The trail follows the treeless ridge past the peace sign that can be seen throughout Missoula. The dog-friendly trail gains elevation gradually. It can be hiked as a loop, returning through Cherry Gulch. The hike has great views of Rattlesnake Valley and Wilderness, Mount Jumbo, Mount Sentinel and Missoula.

Driving directions: From Broadway Street and Madison Street east of downtown Missoula, drive north a few blocks on Madison Street, curving to the right under I-90, onto Greenough Drive. Take the first left turn after crossing I-90. Drive one block on the gravel road to the signed trailhead at the end of the road.

Hiking directions: Head northwest on the unpaved road up the grassy slopes dotted with trees. Just before reaching a knoll is a trail split. Both forks reconnect near the radio tower. The left fork skirts around the side of the knoll while the right fork follows the ridge over the top. Continue on the treeless ridge north, passing the radio tower to a creative fence. A side trail descends into Cherry Gulch along the fenceline. This is the return route. For now, cross through the fence and continue towards the prominent green peace sign. The trail passes along the left side of the sign to the 3,865-foot summit. This is our turn around spot. (To hike further, the trail descends down the north-facing hillside to the signed open space boundary.) Return to the fenceline and descend into Cherry Gulch on the south side of the fence. Bear right at the bottom of the gulch, returning to the trailhead.

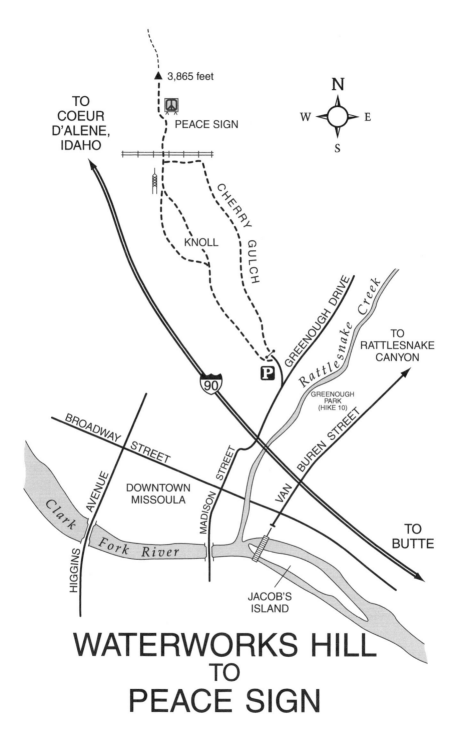

WATERWORKS HILL
TO
PEACE SIGN

Hike 12
Clark Fork Northside Riverfront Trail
Orange Street Bridge to Madison Street Bridge

Hiking distance: 1.5 miles round trip
Hiking time: 1 hour
Elevation gain: Level
Maps: U.S.G.S. Southwest Missoula and Southeast Missoula
Trails Missoula booklet

map on next page

Summary of hike: The Northside Riverfront Trail is in the heart of Missoula above the banks of the Clark Fork River. The path leads through the city parks of Caras Park, Bess Reed Park and Kiwanis Park. From Caras Park to Bess Reed Park, the path is paved and wheelchair accessible. Various side paths lead down to the river's edge. The hike can begin from several access spots. This hike begins by the carousel in Caras Park because the parking is most convenient.

Driving directions: From downtown Missoula, drive to the entrance of the Caras Park parking lot—it is one block west of Higgins Avenue off of Front Street by the carousel.

Hiking directions: Take the paved path west, heading downstream past the carousel. Near the west end, the path crosses under the Orange Street Bridge and ends at the hospital property line. Return back to the east and go under the Higgins Street Bridge into Bess Reed Park. At the east end of the park, the trail detours for a block, looping through a residential area. Signs guide you back to the Riverfront Trail in Kiwanis Park. Head east above the river on the unpaved path. Cross under the Madison Street Bridge to the trail's end.

To hike further, detour up to Front Street and bear right for two blocks to Van Buren Street. To the right is the Van Buren Pedestrian Bridge, crossing the river onto Jacob's Island. The path connects with the Kim Williams Trail on the left (Hike 14) and the Southside Riverfront Trail on the right (Hike 13).

Hike 13
Clark Fork Southside Riverfront Trail
McCormick Park to University of Montana

Hiking distance: 2 miles round trip
Hiking time: 1 hour
Elevation gain: Level
Maps: U.S.G.S. Southwest Missoula and Southeast Missoula
   Trails Missoula booklet

map on
next page

Summary of hike: The Southside Riverfront Trail is a wide, level, unpaved path that extends east from McCormick Park into the University of Montana. The trail was once the Old Milwaukee Railroad bed. The meandering path connects McCormick Park with Clark Fork Natural Park, John Toole Park, the University of Montana River Bowl and Jacob's Island Park above the banks of the Clark Fork River. Various side paths lead down to the river.

Driving directions: From downtown Missoula, drive west to Orange Street. Turn left and cross the Orange Street Bridge over the Clark Fork River. Immediately turn right after crossing, and park in the McCormick Park parking lot on the right.

Hiking directions: Head upstream to the east on the wide path. Cross under the Orange Street Bridge into Clark Fork Natural Park. Meander past a wooden footbridge, native plants, beautiful rock work and art sculpture. Cross under the Higgins Street Bridge into John Toole Park and River Bowl Park. The trail ends by the University of Montana at Jacob's Island Park. To the left is the Van Buren Pedestrian Bridge (to Hike 12), to the right is the campus, and straight ahead is the Kim Williams Trail into Hellgate Canyon (Hike 14). Return by retracing your steps.

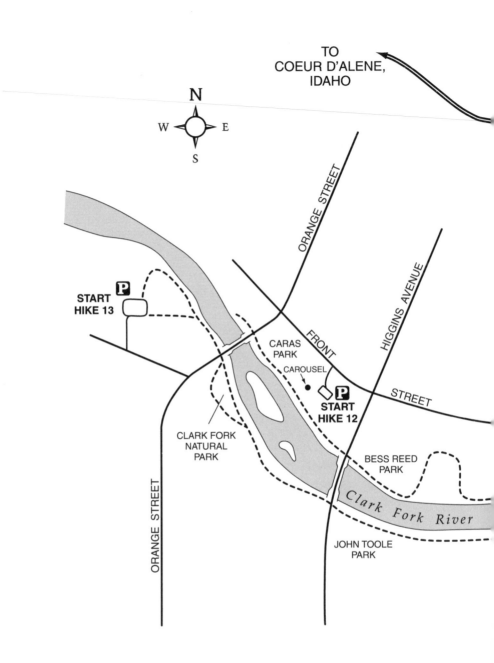

TO
COEUR D'ALENE,
IDAHO

N
W E
S

ORANGE STREET

HIGGINS AVENUE

START
HIKE 13

P

CARAS
PARK

FRONT

CAROUSEL

P

START
HIKE 12

STREET

CLARK FORK
NATURAL
PARK

BESS REED
PARK

Clark Fork River

ORANGE STREET

JOHN TOOLE
PARK

CLARK FORK
NORTHSIDE & SOUTHSIDE
RIVERFRONT TRAILS

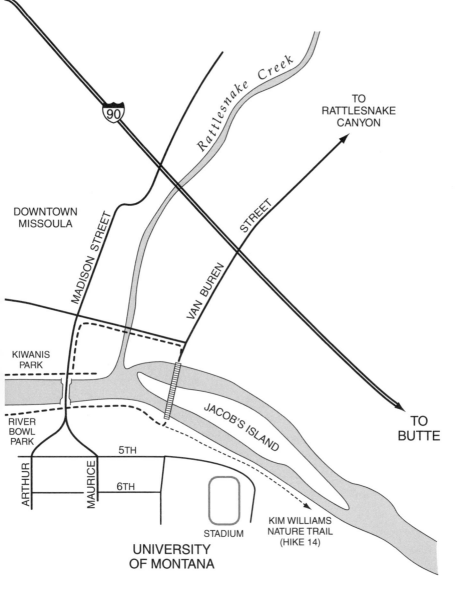

Hike 14
Kim Williams Nature Trail

Hiking distance: 5 miles round trip
Hiking time: 2.5 hours
Elevation gain: Level
Maps: U.S.G.S. Southeast Missoula
　　　　　Trails Missoula booklet

Summary of hike: The Kim Williams Nature Trail follows the abandoned Milwaukee Railroad track through Hellgate Canyon along the base of the steep north face of Mount Sentinel. The wide, level hiking, biking and equestrian trail parallels the south banks of the Clark Fork River beginning at Jacob's Island Park by the Van Buren Pedestrian Bridge.

Driving directions: Park south of the Clark Fork River by the University of Montana, one block east of Maurice Avenue (see map). During the school year, this parking lot may be full. If so, park near Van Buren Street north of the Clark Fork River. Cross the Van Buren Pedestrian Bridge over the river by Jacob's Island Park.

Hiking directions: The well-defined trail heads east along the south side of the Clark Fork River. To the west is the Southside Riverfront Trail (Hike 13). Once past the vehicle-restricting gate, the trail enters Hellgate Canyon along the base of Mount Sentinel. At one mile is a junction with the Hellgate Canyon Trail on the right (Hike 15). Continue straight ahead, following the Clark Fork River upstream. To the left are several narrow forested side paths that parallel and reconnect with the Kim Williams Trail. Various fisherman trails lead down to the water. The trail ends just beyond the railroad bridge spanning the river. Return along the same trail.

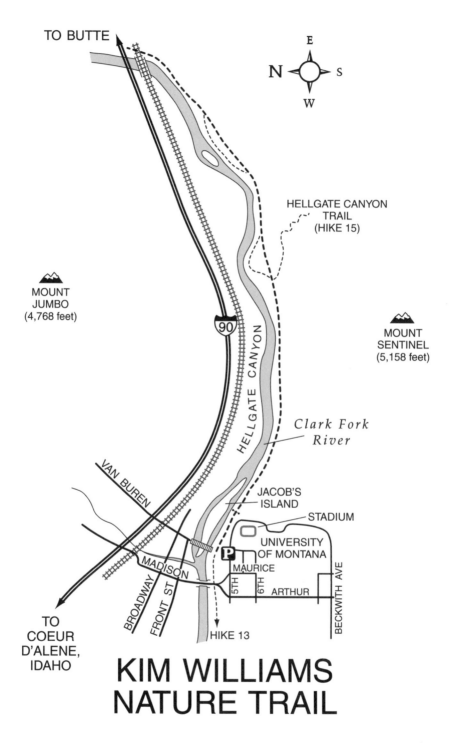

TO BUTTE

E
N — S
W

HELLGATE CANYON
TRAIL
(HIKE 15)

MOUNT
JUMBO
(4,768 feet)

MOUNT
SENTINEL
(5,158 feet)

HELLGATE CANYON

Clark Fork
River

VAN BUREN

JACOB'S
ISLAND

STADIUM

P

UNIVERSITY
OF MONTANA

MADISON

MAURICE

5TH

6TH

BECKWITH AVE

BROADWAY

FRONT ST

ARTHUR

TO
COEUR
D'ALENE,
IDAHO

HIKE 13

KIM WILLIAMS
NATURE TRAIL

Hike 15
Hellgate Canyon—Mount Sentinel Loop

Hiking distance: 6 mile loop
Hiking time: 3 hours
Elevation gain: 1,950 feet
Maps: U.S.G.S. Southeast Missoula
Pattee Canyon Recreation Area map

Summary of hike: The hike up Hellgate Canyon begins by the University of Montana along the Kim Williams Nature Trail, an abandoned railroad bed on the banks of the Clark Fork River. The trail climbs 2.5 miles up the forested north face of Hellgate Canyon, gaining 1,600 feet before the final ascent of Mount Sentinel at 5,158 feet. From the top, the entire Missoula Valley area is within view.

Driving directions: Park south of the Clark Fork River by the University of Montana, one block east of Maurice Avenue (see map). During the school year, this parking lot may be full. If so, park near Van Buren Street north of the Clark Fork River. Cross the Van Buren Pedestrian Bridge over the river by Jacob's Island Park.

Hiking directions: Begin along the well-defined Kim Williams Nature Trail and head east, parallel to the Clark Fork River. At one mile is a junction with the Hellgate Canyon Trail on the right. Take this trail up the switchbacks. The well-groomed trail is not steep, but it goes steadily uphill. The higher you climb, the more dynamic the views. At 3.5 miles—at the top of the canyon—is a junction with the Crazy Canyon Trail (Hike 17). Take a sharp right for the final quarter mile ascent to the top of Mount Sentinel. The trail crisscrosses its way to the top. After resting, relaxing and taking in the views, follow the path one mile down the west face of Mount Sentinel to the "M." From here, the trail steeply zigzags down to the university. At the bottom, head to the right through the university, back towards the Clark Fork River and the trailhead.

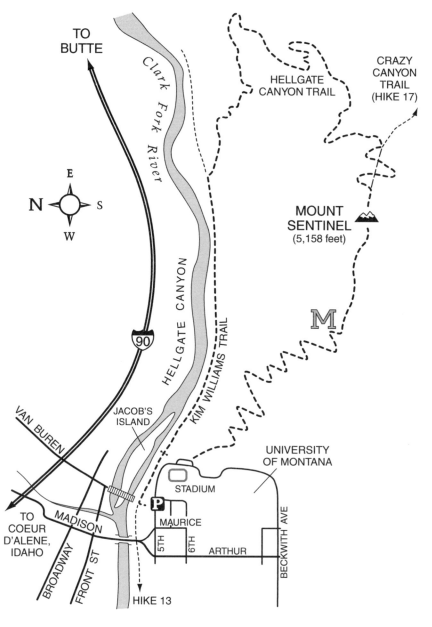

HELLGATE CANYON – MOUNT SENTINEL LOOP

Hike 16
M Trail

Hiking distance: 1.5 miles round trip
Hiking time: 1 hour
Elevation gain: 620 feet
Maps: U.S.G.S. Southeast Missoula
Trails Missoula booklet

Summary of hike: The M Trail is a popular trail with a steady stream of hikers throughout the day. The trail begins at the University of Montana. Thirteen switchbacks zigzag up the sunny west face of Mount Sentinel. From the "M" are great bird's-eye views of Missoula, the valley, the Clark Fork and Bitterroot Rivers, and the surrounding mountains.

Driving directions: From I-90 in Missoula, take the Van Buren Street exit and head south to Broadway—turn right. Head a short distance east to Madison Street and turn left, crossing the bridge over the Clark Fork River. Curving onto Arthur, turn left at 6th Street into the University of Montana. Follow the one-way street curving around to the south side of Washington Grizzly Stadium. The trailhead parking lot is on the left.

Hiking directions: Walk up the steps to the east by the trailhead gate and kiosk. Bear right and begin the steady ascent, zigzagging up the mountain to the concrete "M." After enjoying the great views, descend along the same path.

To hike further, the trail ascends Mount Sentinel to the summit at 5,158 feet. From the summit, trails lead north down Hellgate Canyon (Hike 15) and south to Pattee Canyon (Hike 17).

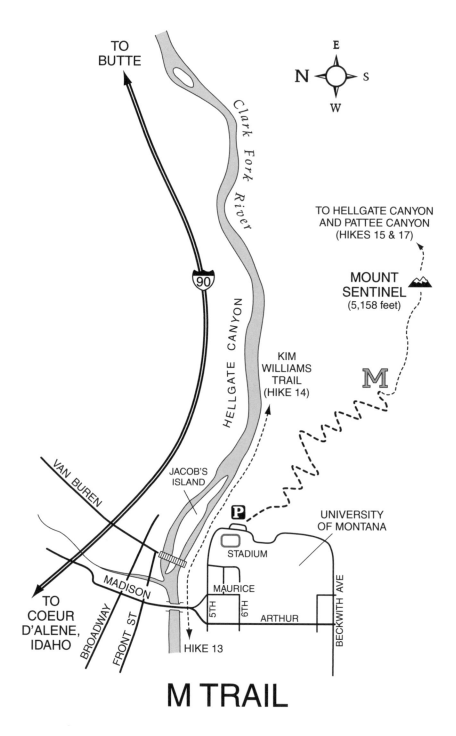

M TRAIL

Hike 17
Crazy Canyon Trail to Mount Sentinel
Pattee Canyon Recreation Area

Hiking distance: 7 miles round trip
Hiking time: 3.5 hours
Elevation gain: 1,150 feet
Maps: U.S.G.S. Southeast Missoula
Pattee Canyon Recreation Area map
Trails Missoula booklet

Summary of hike: The Crazy Canyon Trail begins in the Pattee Canyon Recreation Area. The trail follows a road through Crazy Canyon in the Lolo Forest to the summit of Mount Sentinel, the 5,158-foot peak above the University of Montana. From Mount Sentinel are 360-degree views of the surrounding mountains and the entire Missoula Valley. For a one-way 5.5-mile hike, leave a shuttle car by the university.

Driving directions: From downtown Missoula, drive 2 miles south on Higgins Avenue to Pattee Canyon Road and turn left. Continue 3.4 miles to the Crazy Canyon trailhead parking lot on the left.

Hiking directions: From the parking lot, the trail begins to the north. Take the right fork uphill through the forest to a vehicle restricted road. Take the road to the left. The trail follows the road most of the way. Stay on the road rather than veering off on the various footpaths. At 1.7 miles, the trail crosses Crazy Canyon curving to the left (west). At three miles is a junction with the Hellgate Canyon Trail (Hike 5). Leave the road, taking the footpath towards Mount Sentinel. The foot-path switchbacks up the ridge, crossing the road several times before rejoining it for the final ascent. After savoring the views, return by retracing your steps. If there is a shuttle car at the university, begin the 1.7-mile descent, passing the "M" on the way down.

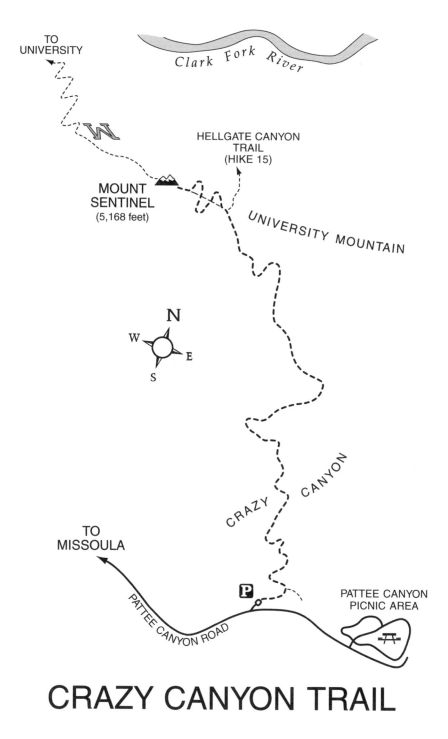

TO
UNIVERSITY

Clark Fork River

HELLGATE CANYON
TRAIL
(HIKE 15)

MOUNT
SENTINEL
(5,168 feet)

UNIVERSITY MOUNTAIN

N
W E
S

CRAZY CANYON

TO
MISSOULA

P

PATTEE CANYON
PICNIC AREA

PATTEE CANYON ROAD

CRAZY CANYON TRAIL

Hike 18
Meadow Loop Trail
Pattee Canyon Recreation Area

Hiking distance: 2.2 mile loop
Hiking time: 1 hour
Elevation gain: 100 feet
Maps: U.S.G.S. Southeast Missoula
Pattee Canyon Recreation Area map
Trails Missoula booklet

Summary of hike: The Meadow Loop Trail is on the north side of the Pattee Canyon Picnic Area. The hike has a network of unsigned, interconnecting trails that loop through beautiful sloping meadows and shady ponderosa pine forests. During the winter, the Meadow Loop Trail is a groomed cross-country ski trail.

Driving directions: From downtown Missoula, drive 2 miles south on Higgins Avenue to Pattee Canyon Road and turn left. Continue 3.9 miles to the Pattee Canyon Picnic Ground on the left. Turn left and drive 0.3 miles to the Group Site parking area on the left.

Hiking directions: From the parking area, hike north past the picnic tables into the open meadow. Several spur trails lead from the parking area to the Meadow Loop Trail. At 300 yards is an unsigned junction. Take the left route, heading west to the west edge of the meadow. The trail curves to the right into the ponderosa pine woodland. Head north through the trees as the trail curves to the east. Along the way there are several unsigned trail forks. These trails all interconnect and lead back down the meadow to the picnic area and trailhead.

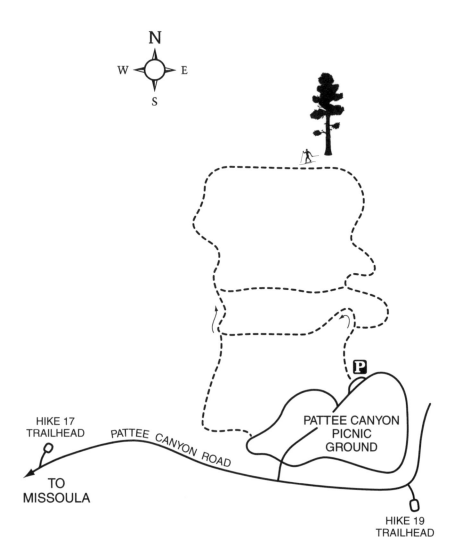

MEADOW LOOP

Hike 19
Sam Braxton National Recreation Trail
Pattee Canyon Recreation Area

Hiking distance: 3.4 mile loop
Hiking time: 1.5 hours
Elevation gain: 350 feet
Maps: U.S.G.S. Southeast Missoula
Pattee Canyon Recreation Area map
Trails Missoula booklet

Summary of hike: The Sam Braxton Trail is located in the Pattee Canyon Recreation Area, four miles southeast of Missoula. The area is an old homestead named after a well-known local skier and outdoorsman. The trail is a winding, curving trail looping through a forest of large, old growth western larch and ponderosa pine trees. In the winter, Pattee Canyon is a popular cross-country ski area with natural and groomed trails.

Driving directions: From downtown Missoula, drive 2 miles south on Higgins Avenue to Pattee Canyon Road and turn left. Continue 4.2 miles to the Sam Braxton trailhead parking lot on the right.

Hiking directions: From the parking lot, hike south past the gate to the posted trailhead. Bear to the right 0.1 mile to a junction. Take the posted Sam Braxton Recreational Trail to the left, winding gently uphill. The trail winds through the forest like a maze. At times it will seem confusing due to old logging paths that crisscross through the area. At any of the unmarked junctions, follow the direction arrows or the National Recreation Trail insignia on the trees. When you least expect it, the trail completes the loop back to the trailhead.

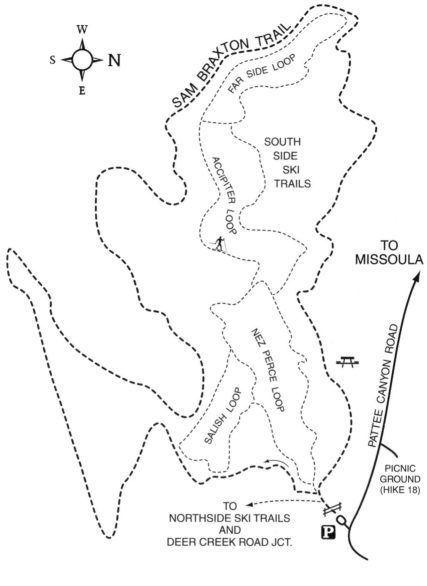

SAM BRAXTON
NATIONAL RECREATION
TRAIL

Hike 20
Vista Point Loop
Blue Mountain Recreation Area

Hiking distance: 3.2 mile loop
Hiking time: 1.5 hours
Elevation gain: 800 feet
Maps: U.S.G.S. Southwest Missoula
Blue Mountain Recreation Area map

Summary of hike: Vista Point is in the 5,500-acre Blue Mountain Recreation Area, part of the Lolo National Forest. The recreation area is located only two miles southwest of Missoula. The hike to Vista Point crosses open meadows and loops through a ponderosa pine and Douglas fir forest. The loop trail crosses over the 4,030-foot rounded hilltop with unobstructed panoramas in every direction. This trail is a popular dog-friendly hike.

Driving directions: From Highway 93 in Missoula, drive 2 miles south of Reserve Street to Blue Mountain Road and turn right. Continue 0.5 miles to the trailhead parking lot on the left.

Hiking directions: Cross the grassy slope, heading west on Trail 3.04 towards the mountains. Pass a couple of intersecting trails while heading to the west end of the meadow and a signed trail split. Bear left and enter the pine forest, beginning the loop on Trail 3.06. Head steeply up the hillside to a saddle overlooking the Blue Mountain backcountry. Curve right along the ridge to the Vista Point overlook. From the summit, descend to the west to a signed junction. Take the right fork on Trail 3.05 a short distance to another signed junction. Go to the right again on Trail 3.03. Continue downhill and bear right a third time on Trail 3.04. The forested path passes Trails 3.07 and 3.08 on the left, completing the loop at the west end of the meadow. Cross the meadow, returning to the trailhead.

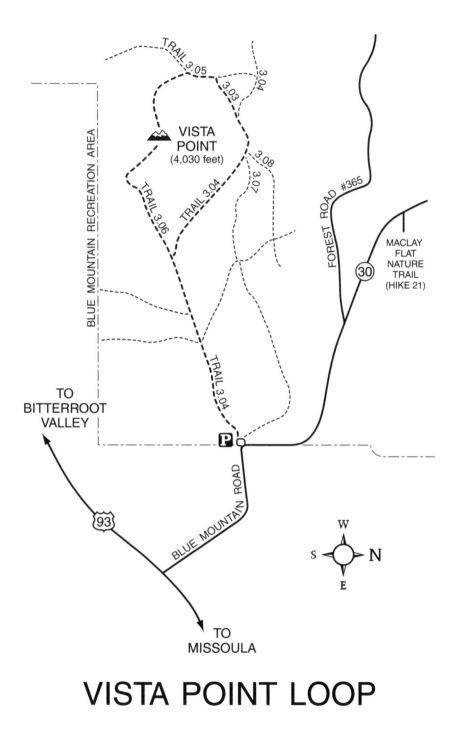

VISTA POINT LOOP

Hike 21
Maclay Flat Trail
Blue Mountain Recreation Area

Hiking distance: 1.25 or 1.8 mile loop
Hiking time: 1 hour
Elevation gain: Level
Maps: U.S.G.S. Southwest Missoula
Trails Missoula booklet
Blue Mountain Recreation Area map

Summary of hike: The Maclay Flat Trail is a wide, level interpretive trail that loops through a riparian forest rich with aspen, cottonwood, ponderosa pine trees and meadows. There are sixteen information sites that describe the geology, river system, vegetation and wildlife in the area. The trail borders the Bitterroot River and the Big Flat Irrigation Ditch on the return. The irrigation ditch is used by farms and ranches through Big Flat before emptying into the Clark Fork River. Benches and picnic tables are available along this wheelchair accessible trail.

Driving directions: From Missoula, drive 2 miles south of Reserve Street on Highway 93 to Blue Mountain Road and turn right. Continue 1.7 miles to the Maclay Flat parking lot on the right.

Hiking directions: From the parking lot, the well-defined trail heads east. Take the left fork, hiking clockwise. At 0.3 miles the trail parallels the banks of the Bitterroot River. At 0.6 miles is the junction with the cutoff trail. The right fork shortens the hike to a 1.25-mile loop. Continue straight ahead for the 1.8-mile loop. The trail curves south and returns back to the trailhead along the north edge of the Big Flat Irrigation Ditch.

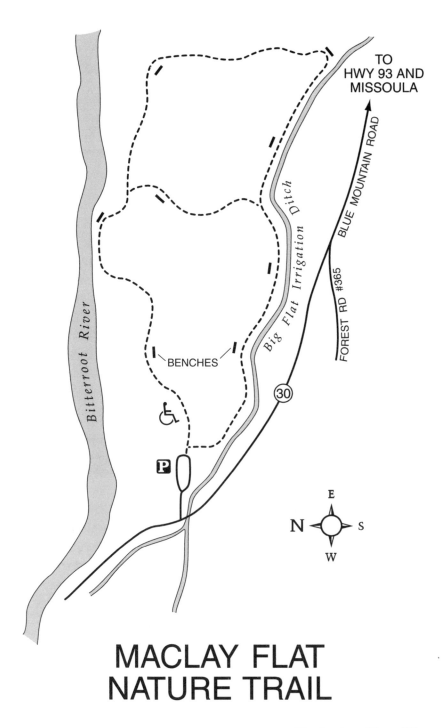

TO
HWY 93 AND
MISSOULA

BLUE MOUNTAIN ROAD

FOREST RD #365

Big Flat Irrigation Ditch

30

Bitterroot River

BENCHES

P

E

N ⊕ S

W

MACLAY FLAT
NATURE TRAIL

Hike 22
Deadman Point
Blue Mountain Recreation Area

Hiking distance: 5.6 miles round trip
Hiking time: 2.5 hours
Elevation gain: 600 feet
Maps: U.S.G.S. Blue Mountain and Southwest Missoula
    Blue Mountain Recreation Area map

Summary of hike: Deadman Point is a rounded grassy knoll at the south edge of the Blue Mountain Recreation Area. From the 4,005-foot summit are panoramic 360-degree views of the Missoula Valley, Bitterroot River and the Sapphire and Bitterroot Mountains.

Driving directions: From Highway 93 in Missoula, drive 2 miles south of Reserve Street to Blue Mountain Road and turn right. Continue 1.3 miles to a road fork. Bear left on the unpaved Forest Road #365, and drive 3 miles to the signed "Motorcycle Trailhead" on the left.

Hiking directions: Head south from the back of the parking lot on the well-defined middle path through the lodgepole forest. At 0.1 mile is a signed junction. The right fork (Trail 6.04) leads to Hayes Point (Hike 23). Take the left fork on Trail 6.01, descending down four switchbacks to another signed junction. Bear left on Trail 6.02. Descend to Hayes Creek at a four-way junction by a log rail fence. Cross the wooden bridge over Hayes Creek, staying on Trail 6.02. Climb up the hillside to the ridge at a junction with Trail 6.05 on the right. Follow the ridge straight ahead and stay to the left past three consecutive intersecting trails. The path curves south for the final ascent to the rounded summit of Deadman Point. Return on the same trail.

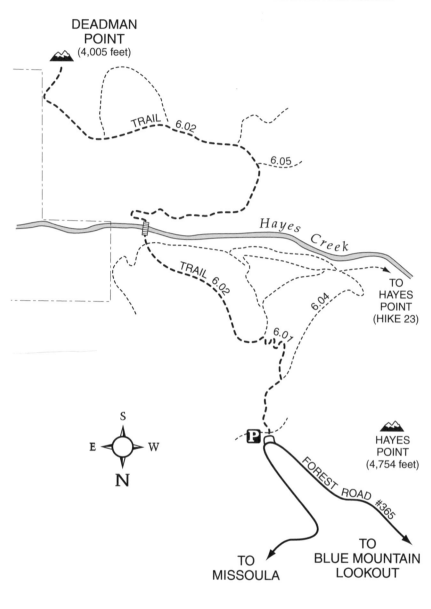

DEADMAN POINT

Hike 23
Hayes Point
Blue Mountain Recreation Area

Hiking distance: 5.4 miles round trip
Hiking time: 3 hours
Elevation gain: 1,200 feet
Maps: U.S.G.S. Blue Mountain and Southwest Missoula
Trails Missoula booklet
Blue Mountain Recreation Area map

Summary of hike: Hayes Point is a rocky tree-covered over-look in the center of the Blue Mountain Recreation Area. From the 4,754-foot summit are panoramic views of the Missoula Valley, Bitterroot River and the surrounding mountains.

Driving directions: From Highway 93 in Missoula, drive 2 miles south of Reserve Street to Blue Mountain Road and turn right. Continue 1.3 miles to a road fork. Bear left on the unpaved Forest Road #365, and drive 3 miles to the signed "Motorcycle Trailhead" on the left.

Hiking directions: From the back of the parking lot, walk through the fence opening, and take the middle trail through the pine forest. At 0.1 mile is a signed junction. The left fork (Trail 6.01) leads to Deadman Point (Hike 22). Take the right fork on Trail 6.04 and continue through the forest. Traverse the edge of the hillside, curving right high above Hayes Creek. Descend to the creek and a four-way junction at one mile. Take the right fork—Trail 6.01—heading upstream. Leave the stream and begin the ascent. The trail is never steep, but it is steady and requires a few rest stops. At the top, the trail meets the road on the left at a trail junction. Bear right and head east to a trail split. Both trails lead to Hayes Point, creating a loop. The more direct route to the overlook is to the right. After enjoying the views, continue around the loop back to the trail split. Return along the same trail. For a shorter return, at the junction by the road, take Forest Road #365 back to the parking lot.

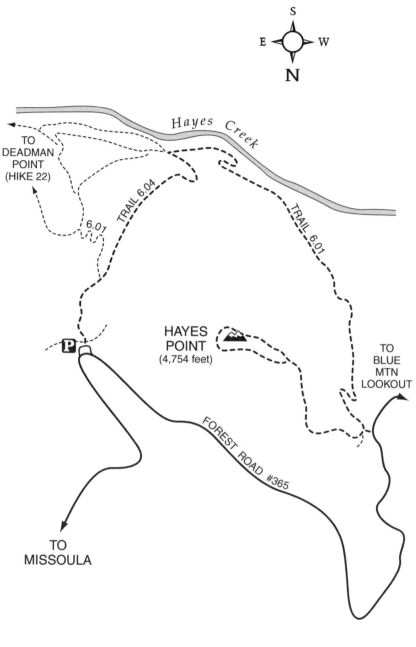

HAYES POINT

Hike 24
National Recreation Trail to
Blue Mountain Nature Trail
Blue Mountain Recreation Area

Hiking distance: 4.2 miles round trip
Hiking time: 2 hours
Elevation gain: 700 feet
Maps: U.S.G.S. Blue Mountain and Southwest Missoula
Trails Missoula booklet
Blue Mountain Recreation Area map

Summary of hike: The Blue Mountain National Recreation Trail is an 8-mile trail from the foothills at the east end of the park to the Blue Mountain Lookout. This hike follows a two-mile section of the trail along a beautiful forested path through ponderosa pine and Douglas fir. The nature trail loop has an overlook with a panoramic photograph identifying the peaks and canyons within sight. Interpretive brochures are at the trailhead and local visitor centers. If you prefer a shorter quarter-mile hike, the road passes the signed Blue Mountain Nature Trail en route to the trailhead.

Driving directions: From Highway 93 in Missoula, drive 2 miles south of Reserve Street to Blue Mountain Road and turn right. Continue 1.3 miles to a road fork. Bear left on the unpaved Forest Road #365, and drive 4.2 miles to the gate on the right at a sharp left bend in the road. Park in the pullout on the right.

Hiking directions: Walk through the opening in the fence on the right side of the metal gate, and head east through the forest on the well-defined footpath. At 0.5 miles, views open up across the Missoula Valley. The path descends through the forest on a winding course with switchbacks, reaching the Blue Mountain Nature Trail at two miles. Circle the quarter-mile nature loop on the level meandering path. Return by retracing your route.

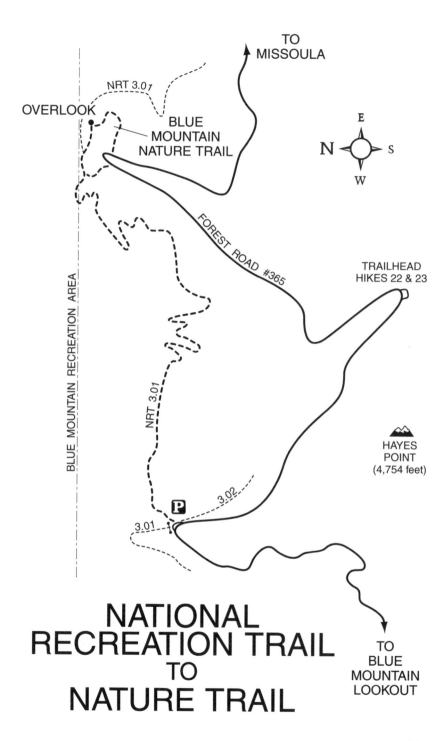

TO MISSOULA

NRT 3.01

OVERLOOK

BLUE MOUNTAIN NATURE TRAIL

E
N — S
W

FOREST ROAD #365

TRAILHEAD
HIKES 22 & 23

BLUE MOUNTAIN RECREATION AREA

NRT 3.01

HAYES POINT
(4,754 feet)

P

3.02

3.01

NATIONAL RECREATION TRAIL TO NATURE TRAIL

TO BLUE MOUNTAIN LOOKOUT

Hike 25
Blue Mountain Saddle to
Blue Mountain Lookout
Blue Mountain Recreation Area

Hiking distance: 2.2 miles round trip
Hiking time: 1.5 hours
Elevation gain: 660 feet
Maps: U.S.G.S. Blue Mountain and Southwest Missoula
Trails Missoula booklet
Blue Mountain Recreation Area map

Summary of hike: The hike from Blue Mountain Saddle up to the fire lookout follows the last mile of the 8-mile Blue Mountain National Recreation Trail. The lookout tower, at the top of Blue Mountain, is a working Forest Service fire lookout. From the summit are incredible panoramic views of the Garnet, Swan, Rattlesnake, Mission Mountain and Cabinet Ranges; the Scapegoat, Bob Marshall, and Selway–Bitterroot Wildernesses; Lolo Peak; and the Missoula Valley. Visitors are welcome to climb the steps up to the 50-foot tower and take a tour during the day. The road also winds up to the fire lookout. The scenic drive to the summit is highly recommended if you prefer not to hike.

Driving directions: From Highway 93 in Missoula, drive 2 miles south of Reserve Street to Blue Mountain Road and turn right. Continue 1.3 miles to a road fork. Bear left on the unpaved Forest Road #365, and drive 10.1 miles to a signed junction. The left fork leads up to the Blue Mountain Lookout. Take the right fork 0.3 miles to the signed Blue Mountain Saddle at a horse-shoe bend in the road. Park in the pullouts on the right.

Hiking directions: Take the signed path on the south side of the road. Follow the grassy ridge southwest toward the lookout, which can be seen above the trees at the top of Blue Mountain. The path straddles the ridge, overlooking the Grave Creek Range to the west and the Missoula Valley to the east.

The wide trail enters the shady forest while steeply climbing the mountain. At 0.7 miles, bear right and follow the switchbacks moderately uphill to the top of Blue Mountain. Bear right on Trail 6.05 (which is unmarked), and walk a short distance to the fire lookout. After enjoying the views, retrace your steps.

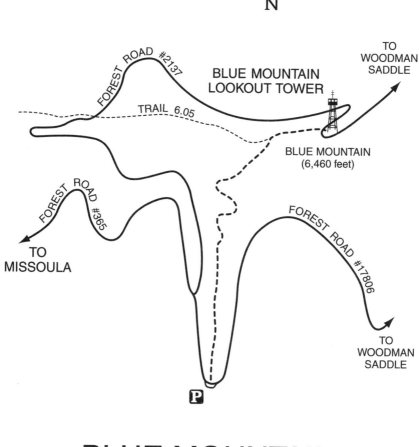

BLUE MOUNTAIN LOOKOUT

Hike 26
Grand Menard Discovery Trail

Hiking distance: 0.5 mile loop
Hiking time: 1 hour
Elevation gain: 150 feet
Maps: Lolo Nat'l. Forest Grand Menard Discovery Trail map

Summary of hike: Located in the Lolo National Forest, the Grand Menard Discovery Trail is an interpretive trail in the Ninemile Valley. The rambling nature trail has two loops that wind through a ponderosa pine and Douglas fir forest. From the trail are views of Stark Mountain and the fire lookout at 7,350 feet. An interpretive brochure is available at the trailhead and at the Ninemile Ranger Station. The inner, shorter loop is wheelchair accessible.

Driving Directions: From Missoula, drive 21 miles west on I-90 to the Ninemile Road/Exit 82. Turn right (north) and drive 1.4 miles to Remount Road and turn right. Continue 3.5 miles, passing the historic ranger station, to the Grand Menard turnoff and turn left. Drive 0.2 miles to the parking lot on the left. Turn in and curve left to the trailhead.

Hiking directions: The trail heads south from the end of the parking lot, past the interpretive trail sign. At the first trail junction, take the fork to the right to hike counter-clockwise. A short distance ahead is a bridge crossing over a stream. Continue to the next fork and again take the trail to the right. The trail crosses another bridge to the west side of the loop. The trail heads south overlooking a large meadow and pasture to the west. Returning back towards the trailhead are two more bridge crossings before completing the loop. Take the trail to the right, and return to the parking lot.

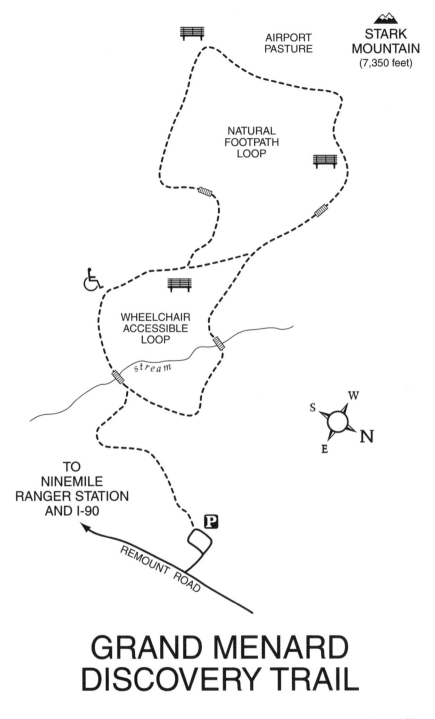

GRAND MENARD
DISCOVERY TRAIL

Hike 27
Cache Creek Trail

Hiking distance: 6 to 10 miles round trip
Hiking time: 3 to 5 hours
Elevation gain: 500 feet
Maps: U.S.G.S. White Mountain

Summary of hike: The Cache Creek Trail is located in the Fish Creek drainage, part of the Lolo National Forest. The trail parallels Cache Creek through a portion of the famous 1910 fire, known as the "Great Burn." The fire spread from Washington to Montana. Evidence of the fire is still apparent. This area is a winter range for wildlife and a fall hunting ground. The drainage gains little elevation for nine miles before ascending Cache Saddle.

Driving directions: From Missoula, drive 8 miles south on Highway 93 to Lolo. Take Highway 12 heading west for 25.8 miles to Fish Creek Road on the right, less than one mile beyond Lolo Hot Springs. Turn right and drive 11.2 miles to Montana Creek Road and turn left. Continue 0.6 miles, crossing the South Fork of Fish Creek, to a road fork. Take the left fork 0.7 miles to the trailhead parking area at road's end.

From I-90, drive 38 miles west of Missoula to the Fish Creek exit. Drive south 20 miles to Montana Creek Road on the right and follow directions above.

Hiking directions: From the parking area, the trail heads west past the Forest Service information board. The trail begins high above Cache Creek. The wide drainage offers frequent views of White Mountain. At 0.3 miles is a shallow but wide crossing of Montana Creek. To keep dry, there is a log crossing 20 yards downstream. A narrow path leads to the crossing. After crossing, take the main trail to the left. The trail approaches the shore of Cache Creek, then strays along the hillside to a second stream crossing at 1.2 miles. The trail leads for many miles into the canyon. Choose your own turnaround spot.

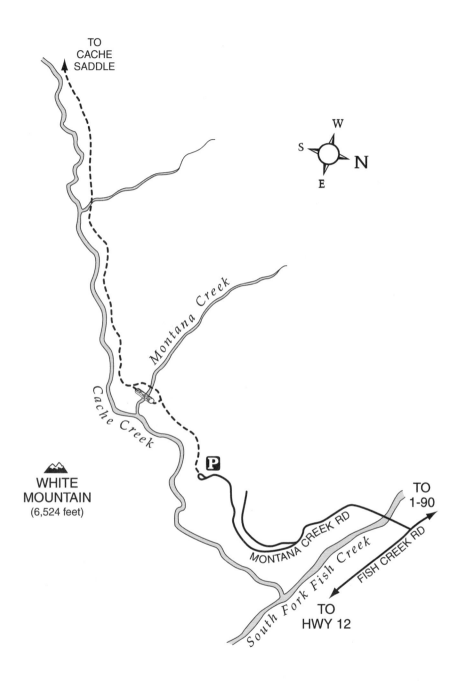

CACHE CREEK TRAIL

Hike 28
Burdette Creek Trail

Hiking distance: 6 to 10 miles round trip
Hiking time: 3 to 5 hours
Elevation gain: 400 feet
Maps: U.S.G.S. Lupine Creek

Summary of hike: The Burdette Creek Trail, located in the Lolo National Forest, provides access into the drainage for five miles, then deadends. The trail follows Burdette Creek through meadows and an old growth forest. Known as an excellent wildlife winter range, Burdette Creek is primarily used in the fall during hunting season. The canyon gains only 400 feet in five miles. There are three walk-through creek crossings.

Driving directions: From Missoula, drive 8 miles south on Highway 93 to Lolo. Take Highway 12 heading west for 25.8 miles to Fish Creek Road on the right, less than one mile beyond Lolo Hot Springs. Turn right and drive 9 miles to the Burdette Creek trailhead on the right. (Stay on Road 343, the middle road, at a 3-way junction.) Parking pullouts are on the left.

From I-90, drive 38 miles west of Missoula to Fish Creek exit. Drive south 22 miles to the Burdette Creek trailhead on the left.

Hiking directions: The trail begins one mile southeast of Burdette Creek. Hike up the forested draw and over the ridge on an old road heading north. At the top of the hill, the road fades. Watch for the footpath veering off to the left. As the trail descends 300 feet, there are great views of the drainage and Burdette Creek below. At one mile, the trail crosses Burdette Creek. The trail then heads northeast up the wide drainage. At 2.5 miles, as the canyon narrows, is a second creek crossing. At 3 miles, the trail crosses back again to the west side of the creek. For a 6-mile hike, this is a good turnaround spot. For a 10-mile hike, continue as the canyon narrows and curves east. The trail crosses talus fields and passes beaver ponds to the trail's end. Return along the same path.

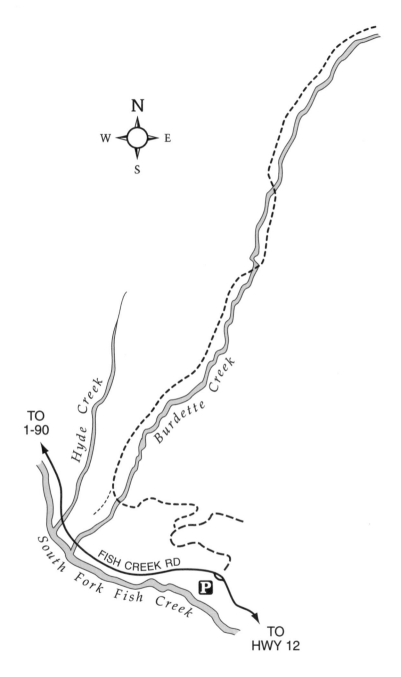

BURDETTE CREEK TRAIL

Hike 29
Lolo Trail from Howard Creek

Hiking distance: 2 miles or more round trip
Hiking time: 1 hour
Elevation gain: 600 feet
Maps: U.S.G.S. Garden Point
U.S.F.S. Lolo National Forest map

Summary of hike: The Lolo Trail is an ancient Nez Perce Indian route over the Bitterroot Mountains into the buffalo plains of eastern Montana. The Salish Indians also used the trail to reach the Lochsa and Clearwater Rivers from the east side of the Bitterroots. The route was used in 1805 and 1806 by Lewis and Clark. It is a portion of both the Nez Perce (Nee-Me-Poo) National Historic Trail and the Lewis and Clark National Historic Trail. This hike follows the original trail along the south-facing slopes above Lolo Creek.

Driving directions: From Missoula, drive 8 miles south on Highway 93 to Lolo. Take Highway 12, heading west for 18.5 miles to the signed Howard Creek turnoff. Turn right and park 0.1 mile ahead in the trailhead and picnic parking area on the right.

Hiking directions: Cross Howard Creek Road to the signed trailhead. Head northwest up the hillside into a dense lodge-pole forest, parallel to Howard Creek. A short distance ahead, a switchback leads southeast, gaining more elevation to a signed junction at 0.3 miles. The left fork descends steeply, returning to the picnic and parking area. Take the right fork on the original Lolo Trail. Traverse the hillside on the narrow, rocky trail high above Lolo Creek and Highway 12. There are frequent dips and rises with a few short steep sections. Cross a logged, sloping meadow through a burn area. At one mile are beautiful rock outcroppings. The trail continues six miles to Lolo Hot Springs. Choose your own turnaround spot, returning on the same path.

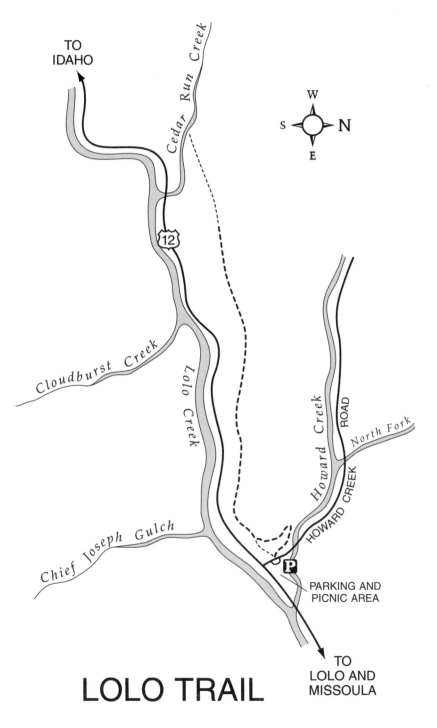

TO
IDAHO

Cedar Run Creek

W · N
S · E

12

Cloudburst Creek

Lolo Creek

Howard Creek

ROAD

North Fork

HOWARD CREEK

Chief Joseph Gulch

P

PARKING AND
PICNIC AREA

TO
LOLO AND
MISSOULA

LOLO TRAIL

Hike 30
Lee Creek Interpretive Trail

Hiking distance: 2.5 mile loop
Hiking time: 1.5 hours
Elevation gain: 200 feet
Maps: U.S.G.S. Lolo Hot Springs
        Lolo National Forest Lee Creek Interpretive Trail map

Summary of hike: Don't let the words "interpretive trail" deter you from this hike. It is a fascinating and informative trail. The hike introduces you to ponderosa pine, lodgepole pine and Douglas fir trees. Then it demonstrates, with examples, the effects of logging, lightening, fire, birds, decay and deterioration upon these trees. An interpretive brochure is available at the trailhead and at the Forest Service Visitor Centers.

Driving directions: From Missoula, drive 8 miles south on Highway 93 to Lolo. Take Highway 12 heading west for 26.5 miles to the Lee Creek Campground on the left. The campground is located 1.3 miles west of Lolo Hot Springs. Turn left, then take a quick right to the parking lot.

Hiking directions: The trailhead is in the campground. From the parking lot, walk up the main road 100 yards to the road fork veering left. The trail heads left along the hillside into a lodgepole pine forest. The trail continues up through the forest to twenty information sites. From the top, the trail winds back down to a stream and bridge crossing. The interpretive trail ends at the gravel road. Head down the gravel road to the right back to the parking lot.

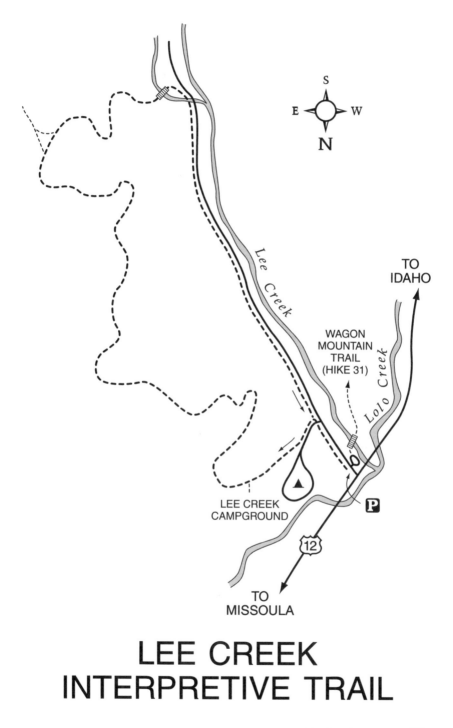

LEE CREEK
INTERPRETIVE TRAIL

Hike 31
Wagon Mountain Trail from Lee Creek

Hiking distance: 6 miles round trip
Hiking time: 3 hours
Elevation gain: 1,200 feet
Maps: U.S.G.S. Lolo Hot Springs
      U.S.F.S. Selway Bitterroot Wilderness map

map on
next page

Summary of hike: The Wagon Mountain Trail is a portion of the Nez Perce (Nee-Me-Poo) National Historic Trail and the Lewis and Clark National Historic Trail. The Nez Perce used this route for thousands of years, crossing the Bitterroot Mountains en route to buffalo hunting grounds in Montana. In 1805, Lewis and Clark followed this route west in their search for the northwest passage. The Wagon Mountain Trail connects Lee Creek to Packer Meadows at Lolo Pass. The hike may be combined with Hike 32 for a one-way, five-mile shuttle hike.

Driving directions: From Missoula, drive 8 miles south on Highway 93 to Lolo. Take Highway 12, heading west for 26.5 miles to the Lee Creek Campground on the left. The campground is located 1.3 miles west of Lolo Hot Springs. Turn left, then a quick right to the parking lot.

Hiking directions: Cross the wooden bridge over Lee Creek, and head sharply up the hillside on the well-defined path. At the ridge, bear left on the logging road for 20 yards and bear right on the unsigned footpath. Follow the ridge to another logging road. Bear left on the road for 100 yards, and again take the footpath to the right. Continue uphill through the forest to an old jeep road. The left fork leads into the Lee Creek drainage. Take the old road to the right, following the ridge separating Lee Creek Canyon from Lolo Canyon. The trail levels out on a saddle, then enters the forest. Begin the gentle ascent of Wagon Mountain. The trail levels out a half mile north of the Wagon Mountain summit. This hike and Hike 32 end here, or they may be combined for a one-way shuttle trip.

Hike 32
Wagon Mountain Trail from Packer Meadows

Hiking distance: 4 miles round trip
Hiking time: 2 hours
Elevation gain: 400 feet
Maps: U.S.G.S. Lolo Hot Springs
U.S.F.S. Selway Bitterroot Wilderness map

map on
next page

Summary of hike: The historic Wagon Mountain Trail begins at Packer Meadows in the Clearwater National Forest on Lolo Pass. Lewis and Clark camped in Packer Meadows in 1805 and again in 1806. This trail is an ancient Nez Perce hunting route across the northern Rockies into Montana. It was also the route used in their tragic flight from the U.S. Army in 1877. This hike begins in Idaho and crosses into Montana. The hike may be combined with Hike 31 for a one-way, five-mile shuttle hike.

Driving directions: From Missoula, drive 8 miles south on Highway 93 to Lolo. Take Highway 12, heading west for 32.4 miles to the Lolo Pass Visitor Center on the left at the Montana/Idaho border. Turn left and continue 1.1 mile to the signed Wagon Mountain Trail #300 on the left, across the road from Packer Meadows. Park in the pullouts on the right.

Hiking directions: Follow the forested two-track road north past the trail sign. At a half mile, cross into Montana to a signed junction with the Lee Ridge Trail on the right. Stay to the left, crossing an unpaved logging road and following the blue diamond ski trail markers up the knoll. At one mile, leave the road, bearing left at a trail sign. Descend on the footpath into the deep forest. Cross a stream and head up the hillside to a logging road. Follow the road 100 yards to the right, and pick up the trail again on the left. Follow the winding path up Wagon Mountain. Near the summit, cross another logging road and skirt the eastern edge of the ridge. At two miles the trail begins the descent towards Lee Creek Campground. This hike and Hike 31 end here, or they may be combined for a one-way shuttle trip.

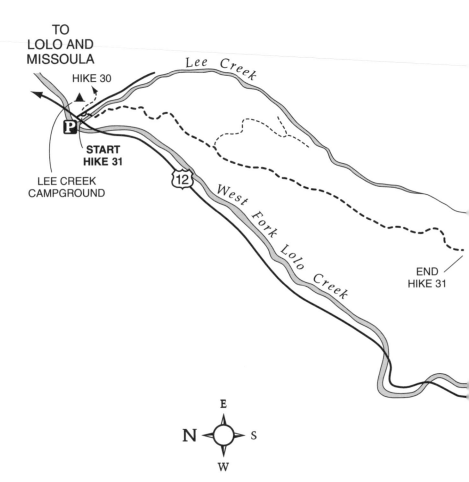

WAGON MOUNTAIN TRAIL
SOUTH FROM LEE CREEK – HIKE 31
NORTH FROM PACKER MEADOWS – HIKE 32

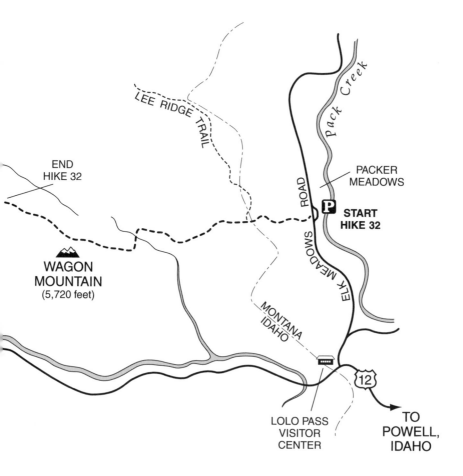

END
HIKE 32

LEE RIDGE TRAIL

PACKER
MEADOWS

P **START
HIKE 32**

WAGON
MOUNTAIN
(5,720 feet)

Pack Creek

ELK MEADOWS ROAD

MONTANA
IDAHO

LOLO PASS
VISITOR
CENTER

12

TO
POWELL,
IDAHO

Hike 33
DeVoto Memorial Cedar Grove

Hiking distance: 1 mile round trip
Hiking time: 30 minutes
Elevation gain: 50 feet
Maps: U.S.G.S. Rocky Point
      U.S.F.S. Selway Bitterroot Wilderness map

Summary of hike: The DeVoto Memorial Cedar Grove was named for Bernard DeVoto, a conservationist and historian. The two short trails loop through the beautiful western red cedar grove where DeVoto edited the Lewis and Clark journals. These massive trees live up to 3,000 years. On the east side of the road, the Trail of Discovery, a wheelchair-accessible interpretive trail, loops past Crooked Fork Creek.

Driving directions: From Missoula, drive 8 miles south on Highway 93 to Lolo. Take Highway 12, heading west for 32.4 miles to the Montana/Idaho border at the visitor center on Lolo Pass. Continue on Highway 12 for another 9.3 miles into Idaho to the paved DeVoto Memorial Cedar Grove parking lots on both sides of the road.

Hiking directions: A loop trail is located on each side of Highway 12. On the west (right) side, take the rock steps down to a trail junction. Begin the loop to the right through a grove of huge red cedars. The well-defined path meanders through the forest and zigzags up the lush sloping hillside. Cross a wooden bridge over a trickling stream and descend back to the trailhead. Several benches are placed alongside the trail.

Across the highway to the east is the Trail of Discovery. Walk down the ramp to a trail junction and map. Begin the loop to the right. The level trail curves left, passing interpretive signs to Crooked Fork Creek. Parallel the creek upstream and cross a wooden bridge over a stream. Complete the loop at the trailhead.

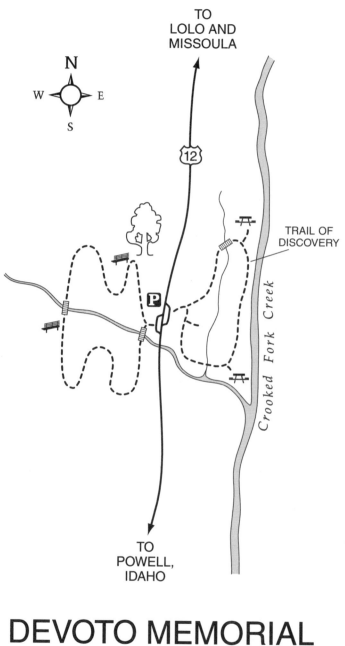

TO
LOLO AND
MISSOULA

N
W E
S

12

TRAIL OF
DISCOVERY

Crooked Fork Creek

P

TO
POWELL,
IDAHO

DEVOTO MEMORIAL
CEDAR GROVE

Hike 34
Hot Springs Lookout Trail
along Lochsa River

Hiking distance: 2 miles round trip
Hiking time: 1 hour
Elevation gain: Level
Maps: U.S.G.S. Bear Mountain and Tom Beal Peak
U.S.F.S. Selway Bitterroot Wilderness map

Summary of hike: The Hot Springs Lookout Trail follows the Lochsa River for a mile. The trail then leaves the river, steeply climbing 2,300 feet to Hot Springs Point. This hike follows the level portion of the trail along the river. The trail begins on the Warm Springs Trail, the path to Jerry Johnson Hot Springs (Hike 35). The Hot Springs Lookout Trail receives little use as almost everyone is headed to Jerry Johnson Hot Springs.

Driving directions: From Missoula, drive 8 miles south on Highway 93 to Lolo. Take Highway 12, heading west for 32.4 miles to the Montana/Idaho border at the visitor center on Lolo Pass. Continue 22.8 miles into Idaho to the paved Jerry Johnson Hot Springs parking lot on the right.

Hiking directions: Cross Highway 12 to the Warm Springs Pack Bridge. Take the wooden suspension bridge over the Lochsa River to a signed junction. The right fork leads to the Jerry Johnson Hot Springs. Take the left fork, following the Lochsa River upstream. Climb a small hill to a signed junction with the stock bypass route to the Jerry Johnson Hot Springs. Stay left and traverse the edge of the mountain above the river. Cross a moss-covered footbridge that appears old enough to have been used by Lewis and Clark. Continue through a lush, tropical looking fern grove and rock hop across a small stream. As the river bends sharply to the left, the trail bends 90 degrees to the right. This is our turnaround spot.

To hike further, the trail begins an intense uphill climb eastward to Hot Springs Point at an elevation of 5,535 feet.

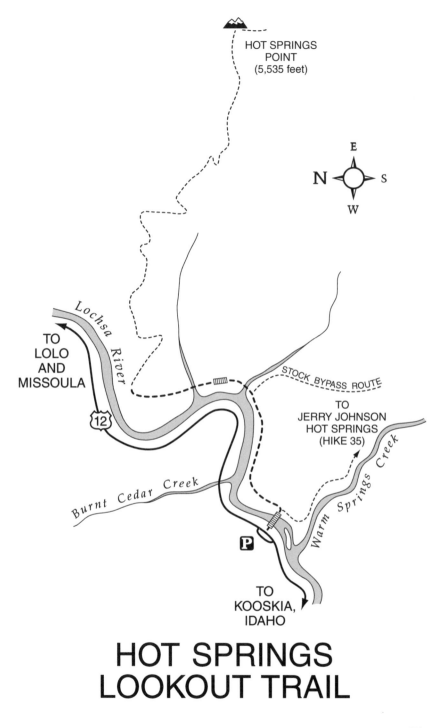

HOT SPRINGS
POINT
(5,535 feet)

N E S W

TO
LOLO
AND
MISSOULA

Lochsa River

12

STOCK BYPASS ROUTE

TO
JERRY JOHNSON
HOT SPRINGS
(HIKE 35)

Burnt Cedar Creek

Warm Springs Creek

P

TO
KOOSKIA,
IDAHO

HOT SPRINGS
LOOKOUT TRAIL

Hike 35
Jerry Johnson Hot Springs

Hiking distance: 2 miles round trip
Hiking time: 1 hour
Elevation gain: 200 feet
Maps: U.S.G.S. Bear Mountain and Tom Beal Peak
U.S.F.S. Selway Bitterroot Wilderness map

Summary of hike: Jerry Johnson Hot Springs is in the Clearwater National Forest in Idaho. The area has a series of primitive pools along the east bank of Warm Springs Creek. Several of the rock-lined hot pools sit beneath thermal water-falls in a beautiful forest setting. A large 10-foot wide pool sits on a hillside away from the creek overlooking a cedar grove. The clothing optional pools are restricted to day-use only.

Driving directions: From Missoula, drive 8 miles south on Highway 93 to Lolo. Take Highway 12, heading west for 32.4 miles to the Montana/Idaho border at the visitor center on Lolo Pass. Continue 22.8 miles into Idaho to the paved Jerry Johnson Hot Springs parking lot on the right.

Hiking directions: Cross the Warm Springs Pack Bridge (a wooden suspension bridge) over the Lochsa River to a signed junction. The left fork follows the Lochsa River (Hike 34). Take the right fork through the forest, following the river down-stream. The path curves southeast, away from the Lochsa, and heads up the drainage parallel to Warm Springs Creek. Ascend the west-facing hillside overlooking the creek to an unsigned junction with a footpath to the right. The right fork heads steeply downhill to a series of hot waterfalls and a half dozen soaking pools at the creek. The main trail continues upstream past more pools. Another side path on the right circles a flat cedar grove meadow along the banks of the creek, looping back to the main trail. Climb up a forested knoll to the last and largest pool on the left side of the trail. Most hikers do not continue past this pool.

To hike further, the trail parallels Warm Springs Creek and reaches Cooperation Creek at two miles. The trail climbs steeply into the mountains to Bear Mountain Overlook and a network of connecting trails.

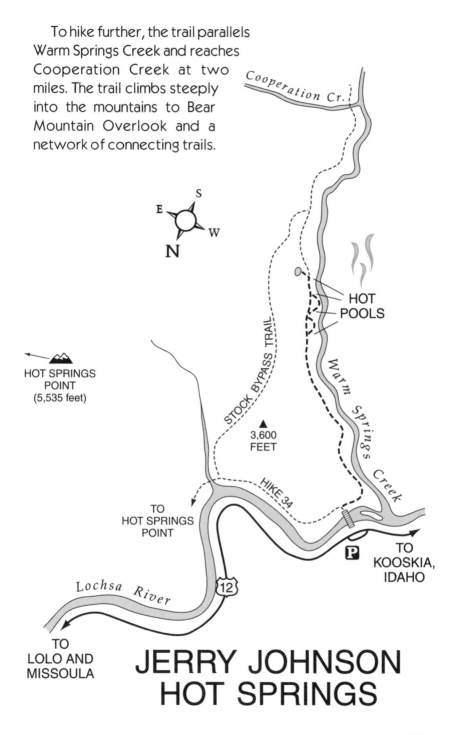

HOT SPRINGS POINT
(5,535 feet)

STOCK BYPASS TRAIL

HOT POOLS

Warm Springs Creek

Cooperation Cr.

▲ 3,600 FEET

HIKE 34

TO HOT SPRINGS POINT

TO KOOSKIA, IDAHO

P

Lochsa River

12

TO LOLO AND MISSOULA

JERRY JOHNSON HOT SPRINGS

Hike 36
Colgate Licks Nature Trail

Hiking distance: 1 mile loop
Hiking time: 30 minutes
Elevation gain: 200 feet
Maps: U.S.G.S. Bear Mountain

Summary of hike: Colgate Licks is an open glade with natural, sulphur-smelling mineral deposits containing calcium, sodium and potassium that attract wildlife. The one-mile loop meanders through the lush forest of lodgepole pine, Douglas fir, Grand fir and western red cedar. The trail crosses open meadows with overlooks of the Lochsa River and Bear Mountain. Interpretive stations describe the effects of fire on the trees and surrounding forest.

Driving directions: From Missoula, drive 8 miles south on Highway 93 to Lolo. Take Highway 12, heading west for 32.4 miles to the Montana/Idaho border at the visitor center on Lolo Pass. Continue 26.2 miles into Idaho to the paved Colgate Licks parking lot on the right.

Hiking directions: Walk up the wooden steps to a platform with a trail map and benches. Take the well-defined path to the right, traversing the hillside past large western red cedars. Continue uphill to a bench and overlook of the Lochsa River, which lies across from the highway. Curve left and head up the shady drainage. The trail levels out and winds through the open forest and grassy meadows. To the south, Bear Mountain towers above the meadow. Rock hop across a stream and gradually descend along the hillside above Highway 12, returning to the trailhead.

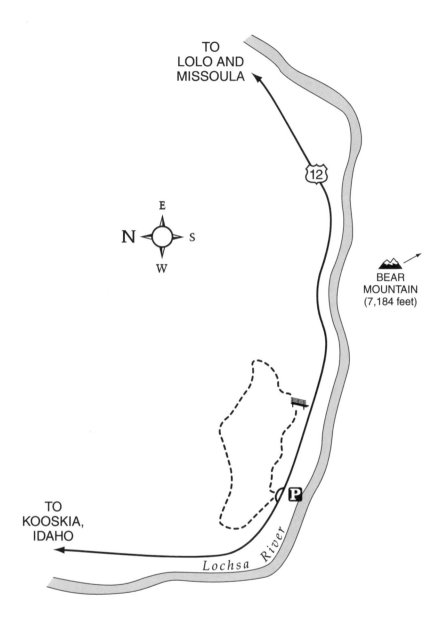

TO
LOLO AND
MISSOULA

12

E
N S
W

BEAR
MOUNTAIN
(7,184 feet)

P

TO
KOOSKIA,
IDAHO

Lochsa River

COLGATE LICKS
NATURE TRAIL

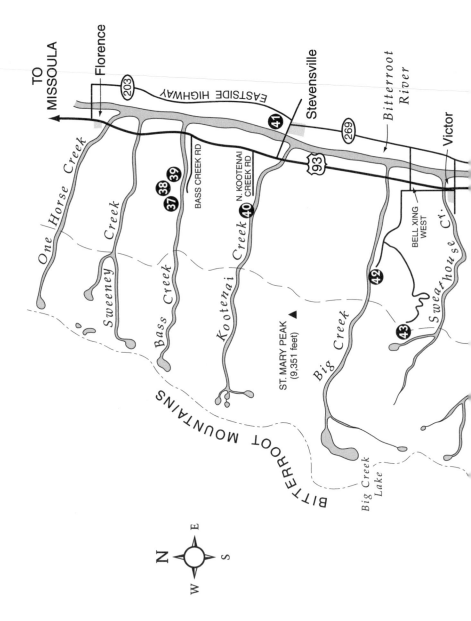

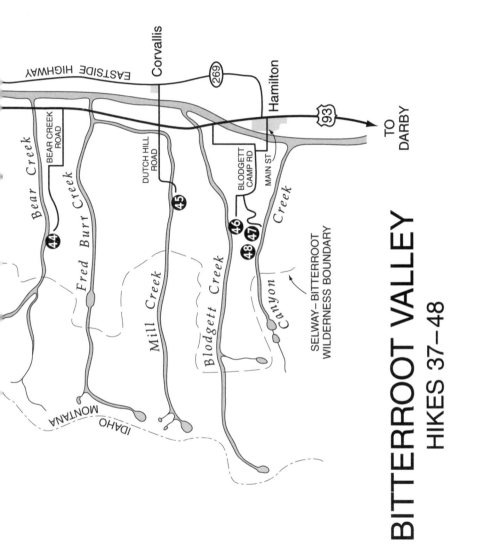

BITTERROOT VALLEY
HIKES 37–48

Hike 37
Bass Creek Trail

Hiking distance: 3 miles round trip
Hiking time: 1.5 hours
Elevation gain: 500 feet
Maps: U.S.G.S. Saint Mary Peak and Saint Joseph Peak
U.S.F.S. Selway Bitterroot Wilderness map
Bass Creek Recreation Area map

Summary of hike: The Bass Creek Trail is an easy hike that gains elevation gradually. The trail parallels the continuous series of whitewater cascades, small waterfalls and pools of Bass Creek. This hike takes in the beginning portion of the trail, heading west 1.5 miles into the canyon to an old log dam. Behind the dam is a large, clear pond. For a longer hike, you may continue up the Bass Creek Trail an additional 5.5 miles to Bass Lake, gaining 3,000 feet en route.

Driving directions: From Missoula, drive 20 miles south on Highway 93 to Bass Creek Road and turn right. Continue 2.5 miles to the trailhead parking area at road's end.

From Hamilton, drive 23 miles north on Highway 93 to Bass Creek Road and turn left.

Hiking directions: The Bass Creek Trail immediately enters the forested canyon on an old vehicle-restricted road. One hundred yards up the road, the trail forks left and stays close to the creek. For the first half mile, large boulders covered with moss and lichen border the trail while Bass Creek cascades down canyon on your left. Then the trail climbs high above the creek along the hillside. As you near the log dam, the trail approaches the creek again. Narrow side paths to the left lead down to the dam. Beyond the dam, the valley widens with great views of the surrounding mountains. To return, take the same trail back.

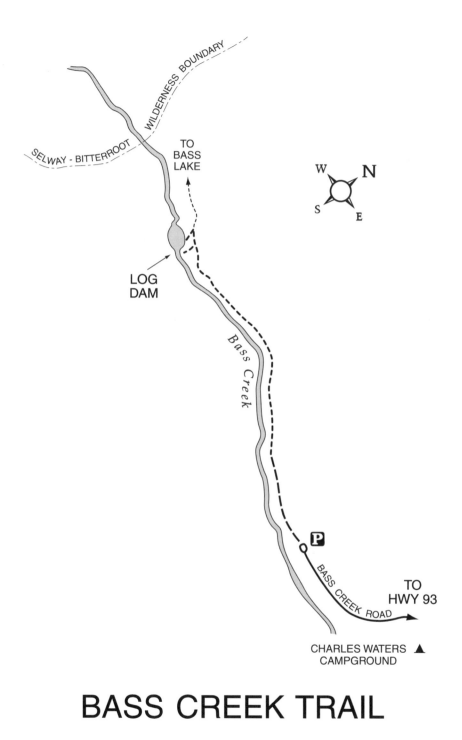

WILDERNESS BOUNDARY

SELWAY - BITTERROOT

TO BASS LAKE

W N S E

LOG DAM

Bass Creek

P

BASS CREEK ROAD

TO HWY 93

CHARLES WATERS ▲ CAMPGROUND

BASS CREEK TRAIL

Hike 38
Larry Creek Fire Ecology Trail

Hiking distance: 2.5 mile loop
Hiking time: 1.5 hours
Elevation gain: 400 feet
Maps: U.S.G.S. Saint Mary Peak
U.S.F.S. Selway Bitterroot Wilderness map
Bass Creek Recreation Area map

Summary of hike: The Larry Creek Fire Ecology Trail loops through aspen stands and a ponderosa pine forest. The interpretive trail studies the effects of fire and the lack of fire on the forest ecology and wildlife. A trail brochure accompanies the hike. It may be picked up at the Forest Service office in Stevensville or from the host at the Charles Waters Campground near the trailhead.

Driving directions: From Missoula, drive 20 miles south on Highway 93 to Bass Creek Road and turn right. Continue 2 miles to the trailhead parking area on the right. Turn right and park in the lot by the information kiosk.

From Hamilton, drive 23 miles north on Highway 93 to Bass Creek Road on the left.

Hiking directions: Walk up Bass Creek Road 200 yards to the signed trail on the right, directly across from the entrance to the Charles Waters Campground. Head north up the footpath. At the top of the rise, the connector trail joins the Ecology Trail. Bear left, curving up the rolling hillside. At just over one mile, by signpost 10, is a trail split. The Loop Trail bears left. Take the Ecology Trail to the right, descending into the canyon. Switchbacks lead halfway down to Larry Creek through a dense forest. Continue downhill to another junction with the Loop Trail at signpost 15. Take the right fork a short distance to unpaved Road #1316. Pick up the trail across the road a few yards south on the left. Follow the path past the horse trailer parking area, returning to the parking area by Bass Creek Road.

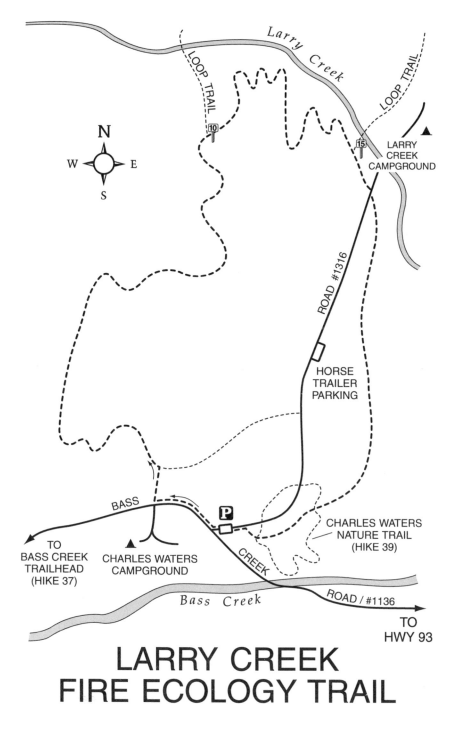

LARRY CREEK
FIRE ECOLOGY TRAIL

Hike 39
Charles Waters Nature Trail

Hiking distance: 1 mile loop
Hiking time: 30 minutes
Elevation gain: Level
Maps: U.S.G.S. Saint Mary Peak
U.S.F.S. Selway Bitterroot Wilderness map
Bass Creek Recreation Area map

Summary of hike: The Charles Waters Nature Trail loops through two different habitats. The hike begins in a dry ponderosa pine forest, then winds through a lush, cool old growth forest. The trail skirts a short portion of Bass Creek and includes two stream crossings. Across the road from the nature trail is a quarter-mile fitness trail with 14 exercise stations.

Driving directions: From Missoula, drive 20 miles south on Highway 93 to Bass Creek Road and turn right. Continue 2 miles to the trailhead parking area on the right. Turn right and park in the lot by the information kiosk.

From Hamilton, drive 23 miles north on Highway 93 to Bass Creek Road on the left.

Hiking directions: Walk down Road #1316 for 50 yards, following the signs to the nature trail on the right. Take the footpath under the forest canopy of ponderosa pines and Douglas fir. Cross a wooden footbridge over the tributary stream. A short distance ahead, the trail follows Bass Creek, then winds back through the forest. Recross the stream to a four-way junction. The right fork crosses the flat forested meadows alongside an irrigation ditch, the return for the Larry Creek Fire Ecology Trail (Hike 33). The left fork returns directly to the trailhead. Take the middle fork straight ahead. The path curves through the forested meadow, completing the loop near the parking area.

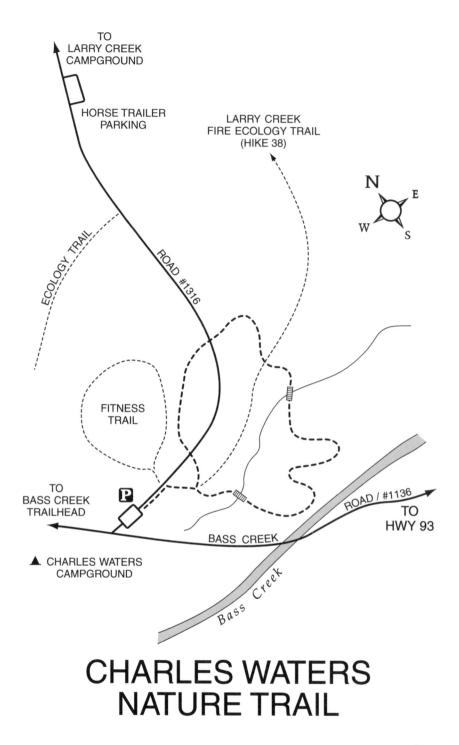

TO
LARRY CREEK
CAMPGROUND

HORSE TRAILER
PARKING

LARRY CREEK
FIRE ECOLOGY TRAIL
(HIKE 38)

N
E
W
S

ECOLOGY TRAIL

ROAD #1316

FITNESS
TRAIL

TO
BASS CREEK
TRAILHEAD

P

▲ CHARLES WATERS
CAMPGROUND

BASS CREEK

ROAD / #1136
TO
HWY 93

Bass Creek

CHARLES WATERS
NATURE TRAIL

Hike 40
Kootenai Creek Trail

Hiking distance: 6 miles round trip
Hiking time: 3 hours
Elevation gain: 600 feet
Maps: U.S.G.S. Saint Mary Peak and Saint Joseph Peak
   U.S.F.S. Selway Bitterroot Wilderness map

Summary of hike: The Kootenai Creek Trail is a heavily used hiking trail for good reason. The creek puts on a dynamic display of raging whitewater, cascades and small waterfalls. The trail stays close to picturesque Kootenai Creek, winding through a narrow, steep-walled canyon. The trail eventually leads to the four Kootenai Lakes that are located 9 miles from the trailhead, gaining 2,600 feet in elevation.

Driving directions: From Missoula, drive 23 miles south on Highway 93 to the North Kootenai Creek Road on the right. The road is located one mile north of the Stevensville junction. Turn right and continue 2 miles to the trailhead parking area at the road's end.

   From Hamilton, drive 20 miles north on Highway 93 to North Kootenai Creek Road on the left.

Hiking directions: From the parking area, hike west past the trailhead information board. The trail follows the north edge of the canyon, always in view of the tumbling Kootenai Creek. There are continuous dips and rises as you head west into the canyon, but the trail remains close to the creek. The trail enters the Selway-Bitterroot Wilderness at 2.6 miles. At 3 miles the gradient steepens. Choose your own turnaround spot.

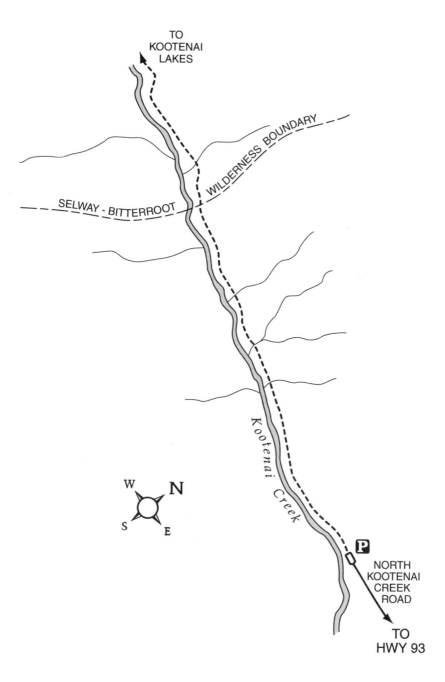

TO
KOOTENAI
LAKES

WILDERNESS BOUNDARY

SELWAY - BITTERROOT

Kootenai Creek

W N
S E

P

NORTH
KOOTENAI
CREEK
ROAD

TO
HWY 93

KOOTENAI CREEK TRAIL

Hike 41
Bitterroot River Recreation Area
Lee Metcalf National Wildlife Refuge

Hiking distance: 1.8 miles round trip
Hiking time: 1 hour
Elevation gain: Level
Maps: U.S.G.S. Stevensville
      Lee Metcalf National Wildlife Refuge map

Summary of hike: The 2,800-acre Lee Metcalf National Wildlife Refuge is in the Bitterroot Valley north of Stevensville on the banks of the Bitterroot River. The 140-acre Bitterroot River Recreation Area within the refuge has two short loop trails beginning at the same trailhead. The trails meander along the Bitterroot River and Francois Slough through cottonwood and pine woodlands, meadows and riparian habitat.

Driving directions: From Missoula, drive 24 miles south on Highway 93 to the Stevensville turnoff (Highway 269) and turn left. Continue 1.3 miles to the Eastside Highway (Highway 203). Head left and go 0.2 miles to Wildfowl Lane and turn left again. Drive 2.1 miles to the trailhead parking area on the right.

    From Hamilton, drive 19 miles north on Highway 93 to the Stevensville turnoff (Highway 269) on the right.

Hiking directions: Cross Wildfowl Lane and take the paved path over Francois Slough to the trailhead kiosk and map. Take the right fork on the unpaved Ponderosa Loop through the meadow and forest to the Bitterroot River. At the river is a bridge leading to a sandy beach on the right. The main trail completes the loops back at the map. The second loop is a paved wheelchair-accessible trail. Head south on Riparian Way, following the banks of Francois Slough past a sheltered fishing deck on the right. A short distance ahead is a junction with Owl Hollow on the right, an unpaved trail reconnecting with Riparian Way. Riparian Way ends at a loop around a picnic area with a covered pavilion at the Bitterroot River.

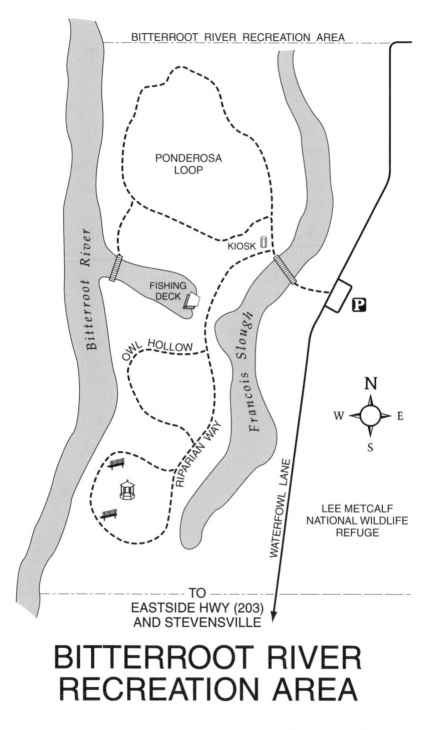

BITTERROOT RIVER RECREATION AREA

Bitterroot River

PONDEROSA LOOP

KIOSK

FISHING DECK

OWL HOLLOW

Francois Slough

RIPARIAN WAY

P

N
W E
S

WATERFOWL LANE

LEE METCALF NATIONAL WILDLIFE REFUGE

TO
EASTSIDE HWY (203)
AND STEVENSVILLE

BITTERROOT RIVER RECREATION AREA

Hike 42
Big Creek Trail

Hiking distance: 4 miles round trip
Hiking time: 2 hours
Elevation gain: 600 feet
Maps: U.S.G.S. Victor and Gash Point
        U.S.F.S. Selway Bitterroot Wilderness map

Summary of hike: The Big Creek Trail is a popular hiking and horsepacking trail. The trail follows Big Creek for nine miles up to Big Creek Lake and dam at an elevation of 5,865 feet. It is the largest alpine lake in the Bitterroots. This hike follows Big Creek for the first two miles of the trail. There are several white sand beaches near wide, slow moving portions of the creek. These beaches are perfect spots for having a picnic and for soaking your feet in the cool water on a hot day.

Driving directions: From Missoula, drive 30 miles south on Highway 93 to Bell Xing West on the right. It is located 5.6 miles south of the Stevensville turnoff. Turn right and continue 0.5 miles to Meridian Road. Turn right and follow the hiking trail signs for 2.8 miles to a road split just past the old mine pit. Take the right fork 1.2 miles downhill to the Big Creek trailhead parking area.

From Hamilton, drive 13.5 miles north on Highway 93 to Bell Xing West on the left.

Hiking directions: The trailhead is at the far end of the parking lot by the Forest Service information board. From here, you are immediately engulfed in the thick, shady forest. Bear to the left and cross the stream. Big Creek cascades down the canyon to the north of the trail. At one mile, the trail crosses into the Selway–Bitterroot Wilderness, then descends a short distance to Big Creek and a bridge crossing. After crossing to the north side of the creek, continue up canyon 0.3 miles to the first in a series of sandy beaches. A side path on the left leads to the beach. This is a good lunch area and turnaround spot.

Return along the same trail.

If you choose to hike further, the trail continues for several miles parallel to the creek to Big Creek Lake, 9 miles from the trailhead.

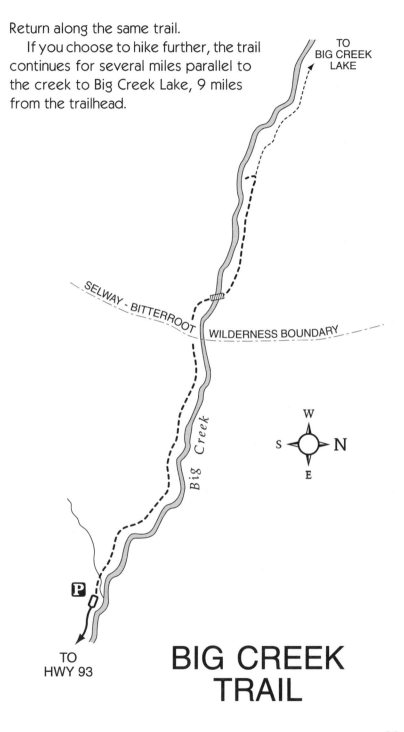

TO
BIG CREEK
LAKE

SELWAY - BITTERROOT

WILDERNESS BOUNDARY

Big Creek

W
S ◇ N
E

P

TO
HWY 93

BIG CREEK TRAIL

Hike 43
Glen Lake

Hiking distance: 5 miles round trip
Hiking time: 2.5 hours
Elevation gain: 700 feet
Maps: U.S.G.S. Gash Point
   U.S.F.S. Selway Bitterroot Wilderness map

Summary of hike: Glen Lake is a beautiful high mountain lake surrounded by steep, serrated cliffs. The lake sits in a bowl below these towering mountains. It is a steady uphill climb to Glen Lake. Rising high in the southwest is Gash Point at an elevation of 8,886 feet. The trail borders, then enters, the Selway-Bitterroot Wilderness.

Driving directions: From Missoula, drive 30 miles south on Highway 93 to Bell Xing West on the right. It is located 5.6 miles south of the Stevensville turnoff. Turn right and continue 0.5 miles to Meridian Road. Turn right and follow the hiking trail signs 2.8 miles to a road split just past the old mine pit. Take the left fork 7.6 miles up the winding road to the trailhead parking pullouts on the right.
   From Hamilton, drive 13.5 miles north on Highway 93 to Bell Xing West on the left.

Hiking directions: From the trailhead, it feels as though you are at the top of the mountain, but you are only near the top. Hike uphill past the trail sign, paralleling the wilderness boundary for 1.2 miles. The trail levels out in a small burn area, then curves west, entering the Selway-Bitterroot Wilderness. The trail descends as you approach Glen Lake. A trail leads around the shoreline in both directions. You cannot circle the lake as the mountains are too steep along the north side. Return by retracing your steps.
   To hike further, the trail continues northwest to Hidden Lake, but the trail is steep and vague.

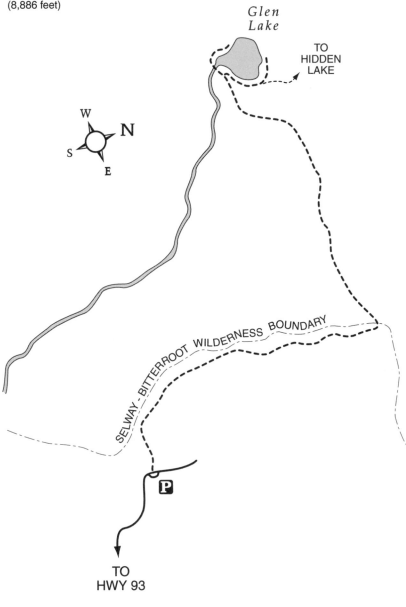

GASH POINT
(8,886 feet)

*Glen
Lake*

TO
HIDDEN
LAKE

W
N
S
E

SELWAY - BITTERROOT WILDERNESS BOUNDARY

P

TO
HWY 93

GLEN LAKE

Hike 44
Bear Creek Trail
to the waterfall

Hiking distance: 3 miles round trip
Hiking time: 1.5 hours
Elevation gain: 400 feet
Maps: U.S.G.S. Victor and Gash Point
U.S.F.S. Selway Bitterroot Wilderness map

Summary of hike: You can easily spend the day at the waterfall area in Bear Creek. It is a playground of whirlpools, cascades, slides and falls. Flat, terraced rock slabs warmed by the sun make great sunbathing and picnic spots. An easy, well-defined trail heads west through the forest to the falls.

Driving directions: From Missoula, drive 35 miles south on Highway 93 to Bear Creek Road on the right. Turn right and continue 2.3 miles to Red Crow Road. Turn right and drive 0.7 miles to a road junction. Turn left and continue 3.1 miles straight ahead to the Bear Creek trailhead parking area.

From Hamilton, drive 8.5 miles north on Highway 93 to Bear Creek Road on the left.

Hiking directions: The clearly marked Bear Creek Trail takes off from the far end of the parking lot. Bear Creek cascades down the canyon to the north of the trail. Follow the trail through the forest, parallel to the creek. After crossing a boulder field, the trail reenters the forested canyon. There is a slight elevation gain throughout the hike. In a clearing just beyond a third boulder field is a beautiful cascade and falls. Bear Creek carves a whitewater mosaic through the rocks. This is our destination and turnaround spot.

For an overnight trip, the trail continues 8.5 miles to Bear Lake and 9.5 miles to Bear Creek Pass on the Montana-Idaho border.

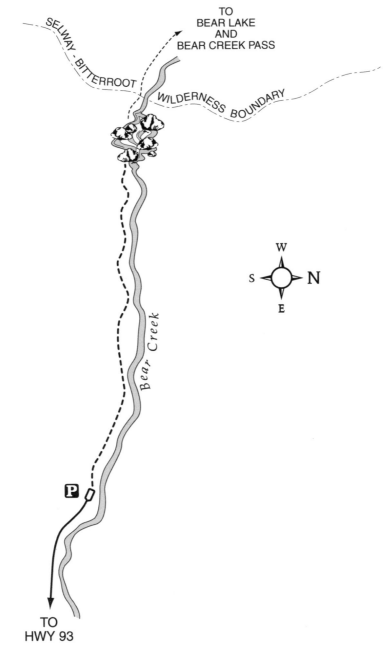

TO
BEAR LAKE
AND
BEAR CREEK PASS

SELWAY - BITTERROOT

WILDERNESS BOUNDARY

W
N
S ◆ E

Bear Creek

P

TO
HWY 93

BEAR CREEK TRAIL

Hike 45
Mill Creek Trail to Mill Creek Falls

Hiking distance: 6 miles round trip
Hiking time: 3 hours
Elevation gain: 650 feet
Maps: U.S.G.S. Hamilton North and Printz Ridge
      U.S.F.S. Selway Bitterroot Wilderness map

Summary of hike: Mill Creek is a continuous display of cascades, falls and pools. The creek's headwaters are at Mill Lake at an elevation of 6,550 feet, eleven miles from the trailhead. The Mill Creek Trail follows the rushing creek all the way to the lake. Soaring canyon walls tower above the trail. This hike takes in the first three miles of the trail to a magnificent 60–foot waterfall and a swimming hole at the base of the falls. The large boulders make perfect seats for viewing the falls and relaxing.

Driving directions: From Missoula, drive 39 miles south on Highway 93 to the Dutch Hill Road on the right. It is located by the flashing yellow light and a sign to Pinesdale. Turn right and continue 2.4 miles to Bowman Road. Turn left and drive 0.3 miles to the posted Mill Creek trailhead road on the right. Turn right and drive 0.8 miles to the trailhead parking area at the road's end.

From Hamilton, drive 4 miles north on Highway 93 to Dutch Hill Road on the left.

Hiking directions: From the parking area, hike west past the information board. The trail parallels, then crosses, a small stream. Mill Creek tumbles down canyon to the north. At 0.5 miles, the trail crosses a log bridge over Mill Creek. After crossing, head left up the narrow canyon. At one mile, the canyon widens, opening up to the sky. The trail enters the Selway–Bitterroot Wilderness at 2.2 miles. At 3 miles, the trail crosses a large, flat rock slab. A hundred yards beyond the slab is Mill Creek Falls. After enjoying the falls, return along the same trail.

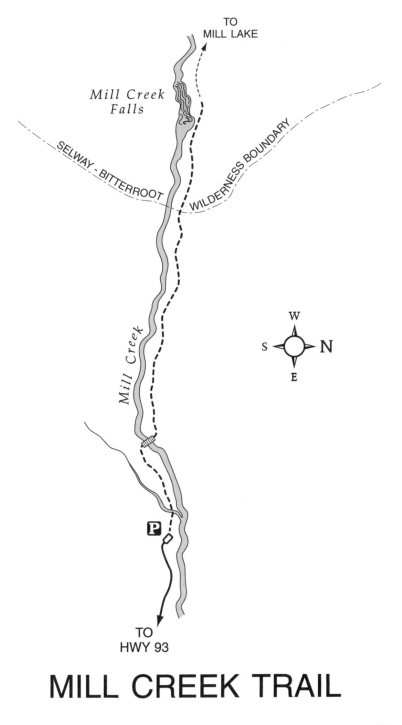

TO
MILL LAKE

*Mill Creek
Falls*

SELWAY - BITTERROOT

WILDERNESS BOUNDARY

Mill Creek

W
S — N
E

P

TO
HWY 93

MILL CREEK TRAIL

Hike 46
Blodgett Canyon to the waterfall

Hiking distance: 7 miles round trip
Hiking time: 3.5 hours
Elevation gain: 600 feet
Maps: U.S.G.S. Hamilton North and Printz Ridge
U.S.F.S. Selway Bitterroot Wilderness map

Summary of hike: Blodgett Canyon is considered the most picturesque of the Bitterroot's many canyons. The jagged peaks of Printz Ridge to the north and Romney Ridge to the south rise nearly 4,000 feet from the canyon floor. Blodgett Creek snakes through the deep canyon. The creek alternates between wide, clear pools and turbulent whitewater cascades. The trail has an easy elevation grade and is well maintained. Although the trail winds nearly twenty miles up the canyon and beyond, this hike leads 3.5 miles to a waterfall (cover photo).

Driving directions: From Missoula, drive 43 miles south on Highway 93 to the town of Hamilton. Turn right on Main Street and drive 1.2 miles west to Ricketts Road on the right. Turn right and continue 0.5 miles to Blodgett Camp Road and turn left. Continue 2.4 miles to a junction with Road 736. Turn right and drive 1.5 miles to the Blodgett Creek trailhead parking area at road's end.

Hiking directions: From the parking area, walk back along the road, crossing to the south side of Blodgett Creek and to the trailhead on the right. There are gentle rises, falls and boulder field crossings along the trail. At 2.5 miles, the trail crosses a sturdy bridge over Blodgett Creek. Continue heading west as the trail levels out and the canyon widens. One mile past the bridge, the trail makes a short ascent to the waterfall. House-size boulders can be used to sit on and have a picnic. Return along the same trail.

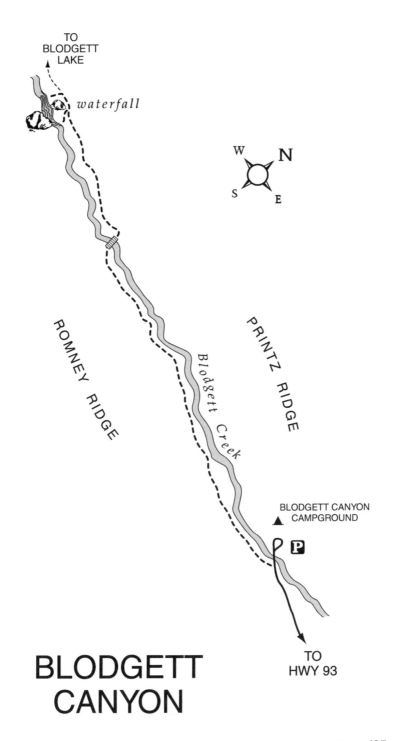

TO
BLODGETT
LAKE

waterfall

W N
S E

ROMNEY RIDGE

PRINTZ RIDGE

Blodgett Creek

BLODGETT CANYON
▲ CAMPGROUND

P

TO
HWY 93

BLODGETT
CANYON

Hike 47
Blodgett Canyon Overlook

Hiking distance: 3 miles round trip
Hiking time: 1.5 hours
Elevation gain: 400 feet
Maps: U.S.G.S. Hamilton North
U.S.F.S. Selway Bitterroot Wilderness map

Summary of hike: This stunning trail begins at Canyon Creek and leads north up Romney Ridge to the Blodgett Canyon Overlook. There are tremendous views throughout this hike. The hike offers views of the peaks surrounding Blodgett Canyon, the Canyon Creek drainage, the Sapphire Mountains to the east, the Bitterroot Valley, and the town of Hamilton below. All of these views are afforded with little elevation gain. Benches are also provided at the various lookout points.

Driving directions: From Missoula, drive 43 miles south on Highway 93 to the town of Hamilton. Turn right on Main Street and drive 1.2 miles west to Ricketts Road on the right. Turn right and continue 0.5 miles to Blodgett Camp Road and turn left. Continue 2.4 miles to a junction with Road 735. Turn left and drive 2.8 miles to the Canyon Creek trailhead parking area at road's end.

Hiking directions: From the parking area, hike to the west 25 yards up the Canyon Creek Trail (Hike 48) to a junction on the right. Take this unsigned trail heading north. There are several gradual switchbacks up the south and east sides of Romney Ridge. Then the trail heads north through the ponderosa pine forest to the cliffs overlooking Blodgett Canyon. At the trail's end, there are many lookout spots and ledges among the jagged peaks. Return along the same trail.

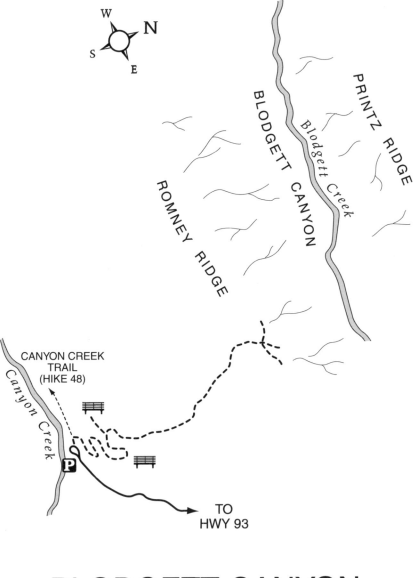

BLODGETT CANYON
OVERLOOK

Hike 48
Canyon Creek Trail

Hiking distance: 7 to 8 miles round trip
Hiking time: 3.5 to 5 hours
Elevation gain: 900 feet
Maps: U.S.G.S. Hamilton North, Printz Ridge, Ward Mountain
     U.S.F.S. Selway Bitterroot Wilderness map

Summary of hike: The Canyon Creek Trail climbs 2,300 feet in 5.5 miles to East Lake and Canyon Lake. This hike follows the first four miles of the trail, which includes some steep scrambles. Thick tree roots reach across the trail along with stable, well-seated rocks. You can hear the creek through the deep, quiet forest, but you will only approach its banks occasionally. Four miles from the trailhead is Canyon Falls, a long, 200-foot cascade off the rocky cliffs. The last half-mile stretch before the falls is very steep and not recommended for everyone. Just before the gradient steepens, the trail passes a small but beautiful cascade with a clear pool. For those who do not want to take on the last half mile, this is also a great destination spot to enjoy.

Driving directions: From Missoula, drive 43 miles south on Highway 93 to the town of Hamilton. Turn right on Main Street and drive 1.2 miles west to Ricketts Road on the right. Turn right and continue 0.5 miles to Blodgett Camp Road and turn left. Continue 2.4 miles to a junction with Road 735. Turn left and drive 2.8 miles to the Canyon Creek trailhead parking area at road's end.

Hiking directions: From the parking area, hike west past the Forest Service information board. Throughout the hike the trail gains elevation moderately except for several short, steep sections. The trail continues through the thick forest, entering the Selway-Bitterroot Wilderness at 1.8 miles. At 3.5 miles the trail heads away from the creek and climbs steeply. Before the ascent, a side path to the left leads to the small cascade and pool. To see Canyon Falls, begin climbing for a half mile. The long cascade will become prominent as you reach the clearing. Although they are not visible from this elevation, East Lake, Canyon Lake and Wyant Lake sit above the falls.

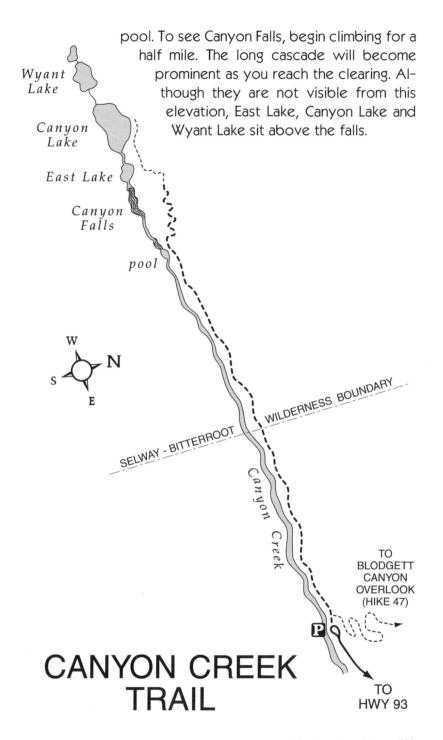

Wyant Lake

Canyon Lake

East Lake

Canyon Falls

pool

W
N
S
E

SELWAY - BITTERROOT   WILDERNESS BOUNDARY

Canyon Creek

TO BLODGETT CANYON OVERLOOK (HIKE 47)

P

TO HWY 93

CANYON CREEK TRAIL

Hike 49
Holland Lake and Falls

Hiking distance: 3 miles round trip
Hiking time: 2 hours
Elevation gain: 600 feet
Maps: U.S.G.S. Holland Lake
      U.S.F.S. Lolo National Forest — Seeley Lake

Summary of hike: The Holland Falls Trail, located in the Flathead National Forest, parallels the northern shore of Holland Lake to Holland Creek and Falls. Holland Falls is a beautiful and majestic 40-foot waterfall. The trail leads to rock ledges, natural coves and sitting areas ideal for resting, picnicking and viewing the waterfall. This trail is a popular access route into the Bob Marshall Wilderness, passing Upper Holland Lake en route.

Driving directions: From Missoula, drive 4 miles east on I-90 to Highway 200 east. Continue 33 miles to Clearwater Junction at Highway 83 and turn left. Seeley Lake is 15 miles ahead. From the town of Seeley Lake, continue north on Highway 83 for 21 miles to Holland Lake Road and turn right. Continue 3.8 miles to the parking area at the end of the road.

Hiking directions: From the parking area, take the sign posted trail south toward the shore of Holland Lake. Twenty yards before the shoreline, the Holland Falls Trail heads east (left), parallel to Holland Lake's northern shore. As the trail climbs and dips along the hillside, you will hike past a beautifully forested island in Holland Lake. The trail curves around to the east side of the lake, hugging the shoreline. There are four log crossings over lake inlet streams. After crossing, the trail ascends 400 feet with a series of switchbacks. As the trail climbs, the views across the lake and of the snow-streaked Mission Mountains to the west are magnificent (photo on back cover). At 1.5 miles, the trail reaches the rocky ledges overlooking Holland Falls. To return, retrace your steps.

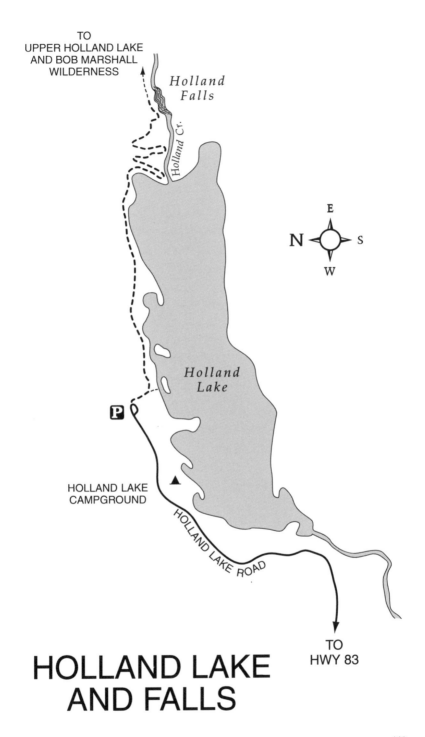

TO
UPPER HOLLAND LAKE
AND BOB MARSHALL
WILDERNESS

*Holland
Falls*

Holland Cr.

E

N S

W

*Holland
Lake*

P

HOLLAND LAKE
CAMPGROUND

▲

HOLLAND LAKE ROAD

TO
HWY 83

HOLLAND LAKE
AND FALLS

Hike 50
Clearwater Lake Loop

Hiking distance: 2.9 mile loop
Hiking time: 1.5 hours
Elevation gain: Near level
Maps: U.S.G.S. Holland Lake
         U.S.F.S. Lolo National Forest — Seeley Lake

Summary of hike: Clearwater Lake, located in the Lolo National Forest, is a rich, blue 120-acre lake completely surrounded by lush, green forest. The level trail circles the perimeter of the lake. From the west shore of the lake are views of the Swan Mountain Range to the east. From the lake's south shore are views of the Mission Mountain Range to the west. Ducks and loons can frequently be spotted on the lake.

Driving directions: From Missoula, drive 4 miles east on I-90 to Highway 200 east. Continue 33 miles to Clearwater Junction at Highway 83 and turn left. Seeley Lake is 15 miles ahead. From the town of Seeley Lake, continue north on Highway 89 for 13.6 miles to the Clearwater Loop Road and turn right. Continue 7 miles on the winding road to the Clearwater Lake trailhead parking area on the west side of the road.

After the hike, you may continue driving along the Clearwater Loop Road 6.2 miles further to another junction with Highway 83.

Hiking directions: From the parking area, the trail heads west through the forest for a short quarter mile to Clearwater Lake. As with most loop trails, you can choose the direction and return back to the same spot, completing the loop. The trail around Clearwater Lake is 2.4 miles and stays close to the shoreline with small rises and dips. Upon completing the loop, return along the trail heading back to the trailhead.

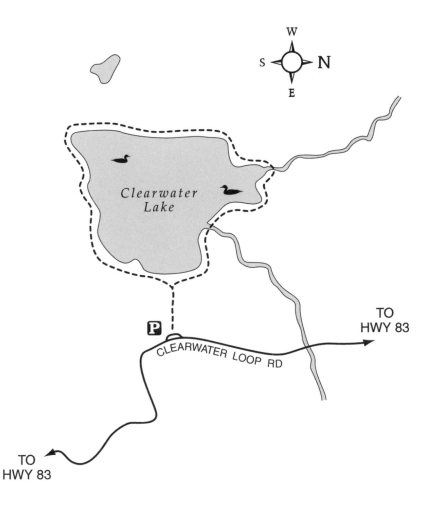

MISSION MOUNTAINS

W
S ✦ N
E

Clearwater
Lake

TO
HWY 83

CLEARWATER LOOP RD

TO
HWY 83

SWAN MOUNTAINS

CLEARWATER LAKE LOOP

Hike 51
Lake Dinah Trail from Lake Elsina

Hiking distance: 5 miles round trip
Hiking time: 2.5 hours
Elevation gain: 700 feet
Maps: U.S.G.S. Upper Jocko Lake and Lake Marshall
U.S.F.S. Lolo National Forest — Seeley Lake

Summary of hike: Both Lake Dinah and Lake Elsina are gorgeous subalpine lakes in the high country basins of the Mission Mountains. The lakes are partially covered with lily pads and are surrounded by conifer forest. The trail winds through lush brush, dense forest and grassy meadows. The mosquitos can be thick in this area, so bring bug spray.

Driving directions: From Missoula, drive 4 miles east on I-90 to Highway 200 east. Continue 33 miles to Clearwater Junction at Highway 83 and turn left. Drive 17.7 miles to the Seeley Lake Ranger Station at the north end of Seeley Lake. From the station, continue north on Highway 89 for 1.6 miles to the signed West Side Trail turnoff between mile markers 19 and 20. Turn left and take Boy Scout Road 0.8 miles to unpaved Road 4349. Turn right and drive 5.5 miles to a signed road split. Bear right and go 4.8 miles to a T-junction. Turn left and drive 2.1 miles to the parking area at the road's end by Lake Elsina.

Hiking directions: Walk a few yards to Lake Elsina, and follow the eastern shoreline to the right, heading north. The path winds through the forest, leaving the shoreline. At the north end of the lake, cross logs over several inlet streams. Climb up a ridge and cross the flat, open meadow with stands of mature evergreens. At the head of the meadow, traverse the hillside over a second ridge. Watch for a junction as Lake Dinah and the Seeley Lake valley come into view on the right. The right fork descends to the southeastern edge of Lake Dinah. The left fork descends to the west side of the lake. Both routes are worth exploring. Return along the same path.

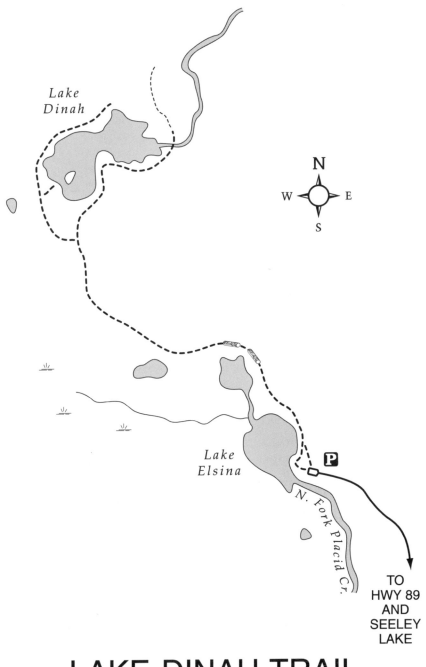

Lake Dinah

N
W E
S

Lake
Elsina

P

N. Fork Placid Cr.

TO
HWY 89
AND
SEELEY
LAKE

LAKE DINAH TRAIL

Hike 52
Clearwater River Canoe Trail

Hiking distance: 3 miles round trip
Hiking time: 1.5 hours
Elevation gain: Level
Maps: U.S.G.S. Seeley Lake West
 U.S.F.S. Lolo National Forest — Seeley Lake
 Lolo National Forest Clearwater Canoe Trail map

Summary of hike: The Clearwater River Canoe Trail is used as a return route for canoeing on the slow-moving Clearwater River. The level trail is a wonderful path through forests and wetlands parallel to the serpentine river. The hike leads to a wildlife viewing blind overlooking a large marshy wetland. The riparian habitat is the protected home to hundreds of animals, plants, waterfowl and songbirds.

Driving directions: From Missoula, drive 4 miles east on I-90 to Highway 200 east. Continue 33 miles to Clearwater Junction at Highway 83 and turn left. Drive 17.7 miles to the Seeley Lake Ranger Station at the north end of Seeley Lake. From the ranger station, continue north on Highway 89 for 0.8 miles to the signed Clearwater River Canoe Trail turnoff between mile markers 18 and 19. Turn left and drive 0.6 miles to the parking area at the end of the road.

Hiking directions: Head south past the trailhead sign, crossing the meadows along the east bank of the Clearwater River. The trail alternates between open wetlands and mature aspen and pine forests. Cross the wetland on a dry elevated path. At 1.2 miles, cross a footbridge to the wildlife viewing blind on the right. Follow the boardwalk to observe the wetland through the blind. Afterward, continue south through the dense forest, bearing right at a trail split. Follow the edge of the wetland past the maintenance buildings. The trail reaches the canoe takeout at the north end of Seeley Lake. A side path leads east to the Seeley Lake Ranger Station. Return by retracing your steps.

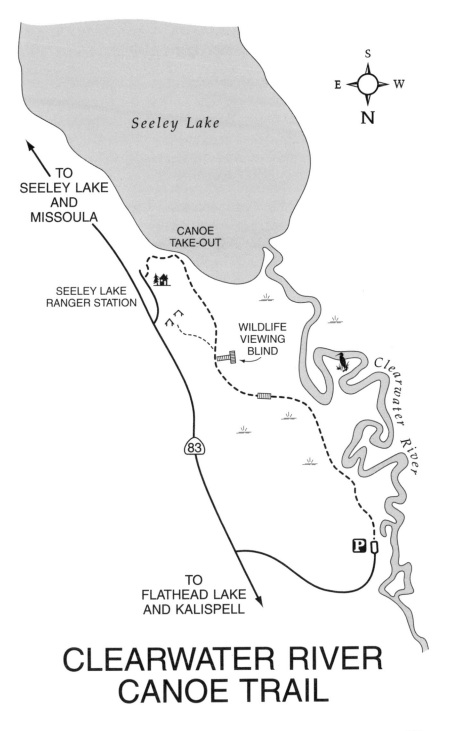

Seeley Lake

TO
SEELEY LAKE
AND
MISSOULA

CANOE
TAKE-OUT

SEELEY LAKE
RANGER STATION

WILDLIFE
VIEWING
BLIND

Clearwater River

83

TO
FLATHEAD LAKE
AND KALISPELL

P

CLEARWATER RIVER
CANOE TRAIL

Hike 53
Morrell Lake and Falls

Hiking distance: 5 miles round trip
Hiking time: 2.5 hours
Elevation gain: 250 feet
Maps: U.S.G.S. Morrell Lake
  U.S.F.S. Lolo National Forest — Seeley Lake

Summary of hike: The Morrell Falls National Recreation Trail, located at the base of the Swan Mountain Range, is among the most popular trails in the area. The rolling terrain leads through a pine, fir and spruce tree forest to Morrell Lake, where Crescent Mountain rises sharply from the eastern shore. Morrell Falls is a series of falls and steep cascades for a total 200-foot drop. From the end of the trail and base of the falls is a stunning view of the 90-foot lower falls, the largest of the drops.

Driving directions: From Missoula, drive 4 miles east on I-90 to Highway 200 east. Continue 33 miles to Clearwater Junction at Highway 83 and turn left. Seeley Lake is 15 miles ahead. From the town of Seeley Lake, drive less than a half mile north to Morrell Creek Road (also known as Cottonwood Lakes Road) and turn right. Continue 1.1 mile to a signed junction. Turn left on West Morrell Road, and drive 5.6 miles to another posted junction and turn right. The trailhead parking area is 0.7 miles ahead, curving left en route.

Hiking directions: From the parking area, the well-marked trail heads east for a short distance, then curves right and heads north. The rolling forested terrain gains little elevation. At two miles, the trail passes a pond and continues past the west shore of Morrell Lake. At the northern end of the lake is a trail fork. Take the left fork, leading away from Morrell Lake to a bridge that crosses the lake outlet stream. From the bridge, the trail curves right to the base of Morrell Falls. Return along the same trail.

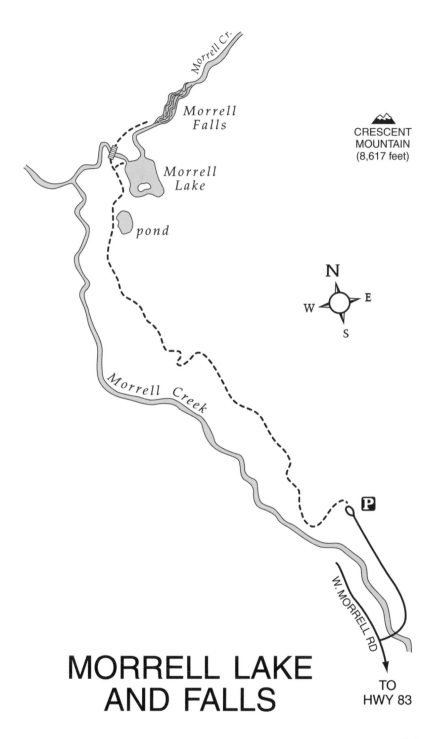

Morrell Cr.

Morrell
Falls

Morrell
Lake

pond

Morrell Creek

CRESCENT
MOUNTAIN
(8,617 feet)

N
W E
S

P

W. MORRELL RD

TO
HWY 83

MORRELL LAKE
AND FALLS

Hike 54
Grizzly Creek Trail

Hiking distance: 3.5 miles round trip
Hiking time: 2 hours
Elevation gain: 450 feet
Maps: U.S.G.S. Grizzly Point and Spink Point

Summary of hike: The Grizzly Creek Trail is a beautiful yet seldom hiked trail. It is located in the 28,000-acre Welcome Creek Wilderness, part of the Lolo National Forest. This remote hike has a deep wilderness feel. The trail heads into the canyon, crossing Grizzly Creek several times.

Driving directions: From Missoula, drive 21 miles east on I-90 to the Rock Creek Road exit. Turn right and continue 11.4 miles to the Ranch Creek Road junction on the left. Turn left and drive 0.8 miles to the Grizzly Creek trailhead parking area on the left.

Hiking directions: From the parking area, head east past the buck fence. The trail immediately enters the mouth of Grizzly Canyon. Grizzly Creek flows down canyon to the south of the trail. The canyon begins to narrow at 0.5 miles. The first of four creek crossings is at 0.75 miles. The creek is small, but you will have to wade through it. The second crossing is at one mile. Rocks may be used to hop across. There are two additional crossings over the next 0.75 miles. After the fourth crossing, return along the same trail.

To hike further, the trail continues alongside Grizzly Creek, but the gradient steepens. The trail eventually leads to Sliderock Mountain at 7,820 feet and several old mine sites.

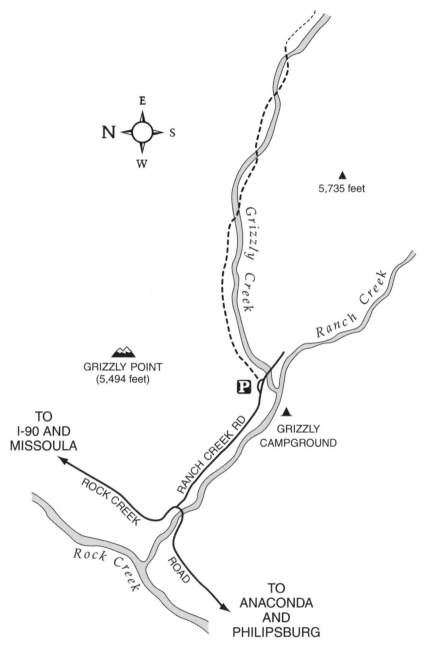

GRIZZLY CREEK TRAIL

Hike 55
Welcome Creek Trail

Hiking distance: 5 miles round trip
Hiking time: 2.5 hours
Elevation gain: 500 feet
Maps: U.S.G.S. Grizzly Point and Cleveland Mountain

Summary of hike: The "Indiana Jones" style suspension bridge, crossing high over Rock Creek, makes the Welcome Creek Trail a hike long remembered. Below the suspension bridge is a white sand beach. The Welcome Creek Trail enters a quiet and remote forested canyon in the Sapphire Mountains. The narrow canyon has fresh water springs, old turn-of-the-century mining ruins and log cabins.

Driving directions: From Missoula, drive 21 miles east on I-90 to the Rock Creek Road exit. Turn right and continue 14 miles to the Welcome Creek trailhead parking area on the right.

Hiking directions: Cross the suspension bridge to the north side of Rock Creek, and head right along the banks of the creek. A short spur trail leads to the sandy beach at the base of the bridge. For a short distance, the trail follows Rock Creek downstream to a log bridge over Welcome Creek. After crossing, take the trail to the left (west) up canyon through the forest. The trail crosses several boulder fields separated by dense forest. There are some nettle plants which will make exposed legs tingle. At two miles, the trail crosses another log bridge over Welcome Creek. Just past the crossing is Cinnabar Cabin and Cinnabar Creek. This is our turnaround spot.

To hike further, the trail continues another 5 miles to Cleveland Mountain at 7,200 feet and the Bitterroot Divide. There is mining ruin at Carron Creek, located 2 miles beyond Cinnabar Creek.

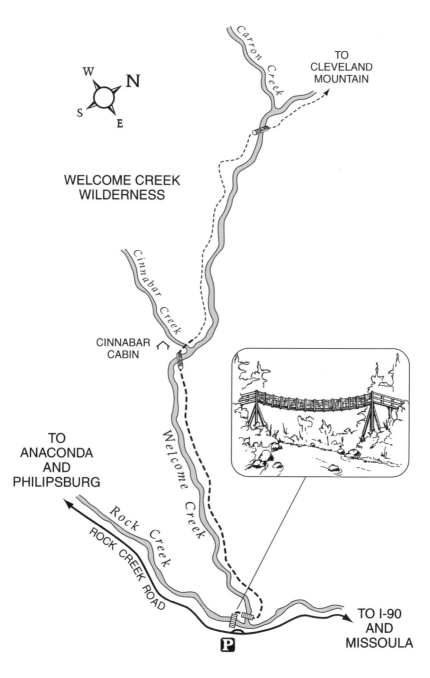

WELCOME CREEK TRAIL

Other Day Hike Guidebooks

These books may be purchased at your local bookstore or outdoor shop. Or, order them direct from the distributor:

The Globe Pequot Press
246 Goose Lane · P.O. Box 480 · Guilford, CT 06437-0480
www.globe-pequot.com

800-243-0495

Notes